A handbook of
PARISH WORK

by

MICHAEL HOCKING

Canon Emeritus of Guildford Cathedral

MOWBRAY
LONDON & OXFORD

© A. R. Mowbray & Co Ltd 1974, 1984

ISBN 0 264 66932 0

This revised edition published in 1984 by A. R. Mowbray & Co Ltd
Saint Thomas House, Becket Street, Oxford, OX1 1SJ

First published 1974

Typeset by Cotswold Typesetting Ltd, Gloucester
Printed by Billings Ltd, Worcester

DEDICATED IN GRATITUDE TO

MY WIFE

Who has always put husband and family first but the
parish a very close second

Contents

Contents

Contents

Introduction

A man and his small son went for a walk that took them past the parish church. They saw the vicar, wearing a cassock, putting up some notices. 'Daddy', asked the small boy, 'what is that man for?' That is surely a question the clergy ought frequently to be asking themselves. What are we for? What are we trying to do? How can it best be done? These are the sort of questions that are posed in this book.

Every parish is of course unique, and there can be no general answer to all the problems that arise. What claims have I to attempt to answer some of them? I can only say that I have been the sort of man you find in every diocese, an experienced parish priest to whom younger incumbents sometimes turn for advice when they do not want to bother the archdeacon or bishop. I can claim to be experienced because I served my title in the East end of London, moved to a new housing area in Devonport, served as a chaplain in the Royal Navy throughout the war years, moved to a country parish in Cornwall immediately after the war, went from there to a big working-class parish in East Bristol and then went to the city-centre parish of Guildford, where I stayed for sixteen years before retirement at sixty-five. Now living in Penzance, it is a great privilege to be chaplain of the local hospital, involved in various local organizations and frequently able to celebrate and preach in local churches.

I have no reason to alter the opinion that I formed years ago, namely that people are much the same at heart wherever they live and whatever their circumstances. Everywhere you find all the virtues and all the deadly sins. Everywhere you find the same sort of ambitions and the same basic needs. Everywhere you find that the Christian religion is able to meet those needs.

Is there an expertise that can be acquired? Are there

certain skills that are indispensable? At a meeting some years ago a man said to me: 'When I was a member of our PCC I attended a meeting convened to inform the bishop what sort of man we wanted as our next incumbent. We asked for a young man, a married man with a family, a good preacher, low church rather than high, a first-class organizer, somebody outstandingly good with youth, a keen visitor, a good administrator and a sound judge of men. We got an elderly bachelor who was high rather than low, a rotten preacher and a bit of a muddler. He was the best incumbent the parish ever had, a saint if ever there was one, somebody who said his prayers and loved his people. He brought terrific new life to a parish that seemed to be dying.' Perhaps the only possible conclusion from this is that saints are not all that thick on the ground. Most of us have to try very hard indeed to acquire the skills that lie within our reach.

It goes without saying that a parish priest must be a man of prayer—and this is a bare minimum requirement. Private prayer, the study of the Bible, meditation, attendance at quiet days or retreats—all this is basic; but this is not the subject of this book. There are plenty of excellent books written by saintly men that will help in the life of devotion and one of the best is still *The Christian Priest Today* by Michael Ramsey (SPCK).

This present book is a revised version of one that first appeared in Mowbray's Handbook series in 1974. It was kindly received and I carefully kept the letters and reviews. Some contained valuable suggestions for possible changes and I always hoped I might be able to use them. Thus I was very glad indeed when Mowbrays asked me not only to update but to rewrite the whole thing. Not only were there several things I wanted to correct. I also wanted to refer to several great issues that are likely to be very much to the fore in our minds now—things like the remarriage of divorced people in church, the possible ordination of women to the priesthood, the new and widely used *Alternative Service Book 1980*, the rapid increase in numbers of non-stipendiary priests and the heavy emphasis necessarily laid on raising seemingly astronomic sums of money to pay our parish quotas. There is one further thing. It just so happens that for more than five years I have been a *Church Times* book reviewer, and among the 160 or so books and booklets I have reviewed in that time very many have been about aspects of parish work. I wanted to include references to at least some of them.

In the first edition I included a long list of people that I wanted to thank for all their help and advice but not one of them would want to be thanked a second time. May I just say how much I owe to the dozen or so men who came to me as deacons and who did so much to help me to sort out my ideas. We discussed everything very carefully. My wife tells me that one of her clearest memories of parish days is hearing peals of laughter coming from the study, when on Saturday mornings the weekly staff meeting was always held. I wish parishioners could know that there is plenty of fun in clergy meetings and that we are by no means grimly severe as we try to serve.

Now in what might be called semi-retirement I look back on over forty years of parish work with enormous pleasure, although sadly conscious of so much left undone. I think primarily of the enormous privilege of it all, the amazing opportunities that came so frequently, the sharing of the happiness and sorrows of so many ordinary people and the sheer joy of what George Reindorp loved to describe as no common task.

Chapter 1

The Parish

(1) *The First Parish*

One of the greatest days in the life of a priest must surely be the occasion on which his bishop institutes him to his first parish with the words: 'Receive the cure of souls which is both yours and mine' followed by induction by the archdeacon with the words 'I do induct you into the real, actual and corporal possession of this parish church and parsonage, with all the rights, privileges and appurtenances belonging thereto'. The parish church may be an ancient and superbly beautiful building that has stood on the same spot for centuries and attracts visitors from all over the world or it could be a Victorian horror that makes the passers-by want to avert their eyes. It may be a small compact village community. Perhaps it is a vast urban conurbation that appals by its very impersonality. But the job remains the same. It is no less than showing God's love to all who will look.

(2) *Statistics of Decline*

The old ideal used to be a parish priest for every parish but this is no longer possible. The plain fact is that comparatively few men are offering for ordination and far more die and retire annually than are ordained. The figures are not without interest. Leslie Paul in *The Deployment and Payment of the Clergy* (Church Information Office), published in 1964, had some disquieting things to say about what he called the statistics of decline. He showed that the numbers of those confirmed, those married in church, Easter Day communicants and electoral roll figures were all moving quietly downwards but at least he was able to point to a steady increase in the number of men made deacon. The figures go up in his tables from 441 in 1954 to an estimated 831 in 1971. What would he have said had he known that the figure would in fact be 636 in 1963 and continue downwards until it fell below 400 in 1971?

This very low figure continued for several years, indeed the number made deacon in 1976 was only 362, of whom eighty-one were non-stipendiary, but after this things looked up again—not perhaps very substantially, but practically every year showed an upward movement. For those who like figures the number of men made deacon in 1982 was 425 (112 non-stipendiary). It should be added that for reasons that will be discussed later standards have not declined in the slightest, indeed they are stricter than before. By the way, those interested in keeping right up to date with figures should consult the current edition of the Church of England Year Book, something that ought to be found in every incumbent's study.

There is ever-increasing emphasis on the importance of faithful lay witness and the effective ministry that can be exercised towards those most in need by doctors, probation officers, teachers and the great army of social workers of every kind. There is a feeling that they do the sort of thing that used to be done by the clergy and there are those who claim that the Church no longer offers a worthwhile job to a man of energy and ability. There is the further factor that the clergy are paid a good deal less than members of other professions. It is a fact of life that most men, including clergy, want to marry and have families—and clergy wives sometimes resent their children having to do without the things that other children, living perhaps in the same area, take for granted. Money and career prospects are factors that some parents take into account when trying to talk their sons out of offering for ordination. One hopes this tendency will not be reversed by present unemployment prospects.

(3) *Numbers of Clergy*

For some reason or other we always seem to get very depressed about the numbers of clergy. Take this extract from the 1927 Crockford preface quoted by Roger Lloyd in his *Church of England 1900-1965*:

> It is not too much to say that if the history of the last ten years is continued for another ten the effective maintenance of the parochial system will have become impossible in all but a few favoured localities. Anything that can fairly be called the Church of England will have ceased to exist and its place will have been taken by the sporadic activities of a denomination.

Yet there are still plenty of clergymen around and quite sufficient to do the job very adequately even if arrangements have to be made that would have caused Victorian novelists to have had severe fits of the vapours.

The figures are in *Church Statistics* (CIO). For instance, in 1982 there were 8,434 incumbents, 1,712 assistant curates, 374 dignitaries and 295 non-parochial diocesan clergyman. There were in fact 10,815 diocesan clergymen in all, compared with 13,185 in 1972. It is interesting to note that according to the Sheffield Report formula (GS 205) the Canterbury province had 1.5 per cent too many and York 3.5 per cent too few. By 1983 we had it very nearly right. It should be added that in 1982 there were over 2,000 other clergymen in non-parochial posts outside the diocesan framework, e.g. chaplains in HM Forces, prisons, hospitals and schools, not to mention officials of charitable organizations, religious communities, theological colleges and universities. Many of them do work that is very similar to that of a parish priest but some do not really need holy orders for the jobs. It is always sad to see priests appointed to jobs that can equally well be done by the laity.

It is quite true that for years past it has not been possible to provide every single parish with its own resident parish priest. Country areas used to suffer most from the shortage of suitable men. A large diocese at any given moment might have thirty or forty vacant livings, many of them tiny villages with vast parsonages. Not surprisingly, few men wanted to take on a job where virtually nobody came to church and most of the work lay in mowing the lawns and keeping down the weeds.

Dr Cyril Garbett suggested one answer in *An Age of Revolution*:

> With the shortage of clergy it was plainly the right policy to group together parishes so that one clergyman might minister to two, three, or even four, instead of each one of these little communities having its own resident priest. By plurality and schemes of union large numbers of parishes have been temporarily or permanently united and thus it has been possible to pay the country clergy more adequately and at the same time to check an excessive flow of the men from the town to the country parishes. The recent 'Pastoral Re-organisation Measure' has given each diocese the power to survey its parishes as a whole and to re-group and re-organise them so that both men and money are used to the best advantage.

(4) *Team Ministries*

In the diocese of Lincoln a better way was found. It was decided to appoint one man as rector of a large group of no less than fifteen small parishes with twelve churches. He covered an area of seventy-five square miles and a population of just over 1,100 assisted by a deacon. Before the grouping these parishes had been served by six elderly incumbents. That scheme is described in *The South Ormsby Experiment* (SPCK, 1960).

In the Norwich scheme piloted by Hugh Blackburne with two assistant curates there were originally ten rather run-down parish churches. Hugh and Freda Blackburne went to each in turn, equipped with buckets and brooms and scrubbing brushes. In no time first women of goodwill and then men were working hard and a church that had perhaps looked thoroughly neglected for years began to look loved and cared for.

One of the most impressive things was a marked return to church attendance. Every parish church had regular services and these began to attract reasonable congregations of local residents. A parish bus collected people from time to time to attend other churches in the group. A united council was formed, a system of priorities was worked out and gradually each church was restored and beautified. All ten parishes would share in a very big annual summer fete and the total proceeds would go to one church in the group. Astonishing sums of money were raised for this purpose and a magnificent job of work was done. Here is surely a positive way of ministering to long neglected rural parishes.

Under the Pastoral Measure 1968, the Great Ormsby and Hillborough experiments are now properly described as team ministries and such ministries may be established by a Pastoral Scheme initiated by the Diocesan Pastoral Committee. There is one incumbent 'rector' of the benefice with other priests of incumbent status having the title 'vicar' and in addition there may be assistant curates. The scheme applies to country or town.

Teams and groups have come a long way since Arthur Smith wrote his survey in 1965. There has been much discussion arising out of the implications of the latest version of the Pastoral Measure 1983, and consideration is now being given to the place of lay members in a team, the advantages of freehold as against leasehold and the ecumenical aspects.

The main features of a team ministry are as follows:

1. The office of rector may be either freehold or for a specified term of years.

2. The first rector may be named in the scheme.
3. The rector is responsible for the leadership of the team and has a general responsibility for the cure of souls in the area of the benefice.
4. The rector and the team vicars are required to meet as a chapter at regular intervals for the purpose of consulting together.
5. A district in the parish having a church or licensed place of worship may have a district church council.
6. When the area of a team ministry occupies more than one parish a group council may be established.

(5) *Group Ministries*

A group ministry is quite different: for a Pastoral Scheme may establish a group ministry for a group of benefices, the benefices continuing their separate and distinct existence. The main features of a group ministry are:

1. Each of the incumbents in the group has authority to perform in the area of all benefices in the group all such offices and services as may be performed by the respective incumbents. When acting outside his own benefice he must act in accordance with the directions of the incumbent concerned.
2. The incumbents are required to assist each other so as to make the best possible provision for the cure of souls throughout the area of a group.
3. An incumbent cannot withdraw his benefice from the group.
4. The scheme may name who is to be the first incumbent of any benefice in the group.
5. The incumbents of the group are required to meet together as a chapter.
6. The scheme may provide for the establishment of a group council.

Much of this has been simplified by the 1983 Pastoral

Measure, indeed it might be said that the only essential things are that a team ministry is one that has a captain while a group ministry is one where there is no captain. Perhaps it is best not to have the original rather restrictive conditions but to leave things to develop in particular areas.

Group ministries are needed most of all in fair sized towns with anything up to a dozen parish churches that may to the casual eye appear to be working in rivalry rather than in co-operation. One might have a brilliant preacher; another an outstanding teacher; a third a first rate administrator; a fourth an exceptionally talented youth leader. No one man possess all the virtues. Obviously it would be a great step forward if all the incumbents could work together as a team so that each parish benefited from the various skills thus made available. But the pitfalls in the way of acceptance of any such scheme are considerable, not least the desire of some incumbents to go it alone.

The Morley Report (*Partners in Ministry*, CIO, 1967) would have removed the difficulties by limiting the freehold, but it was rejected by the General Synod's predecessor (Church Assembly) because parochial clergymen, for the most part, were not prepared to surrender their ancient rights and be appointed only for a term of years; and the laity supported them. Perhaps this is why progress has been slow. By the end of 1982 a total of 316 schemes had been completed for the establishment of team ministries and 77 for group ministries, roughly nine per diocese (accounting for perhaps 10 per cent of the parochial clergy). More are surely needed, partly because the shortage of clergy makes it imperative, partly because of the splendid training provided for junior clergy and partly because by these means the energy and willingness to help of retired clergy can best be harnessed. One of the most helpful booklets about what is often called the collaborative ministry is *A Primer for Teams* by Peter Croft (ONE Publications, 1979) and another useful work is *Tap Handbook for Teams and Groups* by John Hammersley (British Council of Churches, 1981).

(6) *Non-Stipendiary Ministries*

A phenomenon of the eighties has been the growth of the non-stipendiary ministry.* The Southwark Ordination Course pioneered much of the spare time training required by men who, while continuing their ordinary jobs, offered themselves for ordination to the sacred ministry. The Lambeth Conference of 1930 gave cautious approval to what they called 'voluntary clergy' while in 1968 an ACCM Report called *A Supporting Ministry* spelled out the details for the selection and training of non-stipendiary ministers. Now there are no less than fifteen training centres for this form of ministry and they will be found listed in the next chapter.

Something like 125 men are being made deacon annually to serve in this capacity and we can never be sufficiently grateful to those who accept this work and help to cover gaps left by declining numbers of full-time men. But there are dangers. A man who works full time at perhaps an important and demanding job and who has perhaps a wife and several children can obviously offer very little time to the hard-pressed parish priest. If he wants to become more involved in pastoral work, in weddings and funerals and confirmation preparation and so on, then his job and his family are going to suffer. What they are really needed for most of all is the celebration of Holy Communion on Sundays. Somehow we are afraid of the term 'mass priests' because of the abuses associated with the chantry masses of long ago, but the term should not be considered pejorative. A non-stipendiary priest who is willing to celebrate Sunday by Sunday can do an immense amount to help, particularly in a parish where there are several churches and a need for more celebrations than the full-time incumbent can possibly manage. Usually a sermon has to be preached. How does a man manage to preach possibly every Sunday when one a month, considered enough for a deacon to prepare, is probably as much as he

---

* It is interesting to note that in 1971 there were 98 non-stipendiary clergymen in England. In 1983 the figure had risen to 760.

can properly manage? Surely there cannot possibly be any objections to his reading from the pulpit a sermon by somebody else (and of course saying what he is doing). I have reviewed no less than twelve books of sermons in the past year or two; every single one of them contains sermons that would serve admirably for this purpose. I have listed them in the bibliography.

Men who used to feel called to be readers may well feel called to the non-stipendiary ministry now that it is so much more common. The right thing is to have a word with the incumbent, who will get in touch with the diocesan bishop, who may well recommend the man to ACCM for consideration at a selection conference. There is no maximum age at present and each diocese has its own procedures. Many a non-stipendiary priest really comes into his own after retirement, and for some this may well be before the age of sixty-five. A useful booklet about the non-stipendiary ministry called *Training for Diversity in Ministry* (University of Nottingham) was published in 1983.

(7) *Types of Parish*

What are the different types of parish and what are their characteristic problems? Leslie Paul states in his Report that in 1961 there were 939 parishes with populations between 10,000 and 19,999, 116 with populations over 20,000 and only one parish of over 50,000. No doubt there are slightly more of these larger parishes now. On the other hand, 65 per cent of the parishes in this land are rural with populations of under 500.

Parishes might be classified as follows:

(a) The Small Country Parish

The incumbent really must be a countryman himself with a great love for country things and country ways. If he hates the smell of pigs and is allergic to new mown hay he had better go somewhere else. The tempo of country life is slower but the amount of work to be done is as big or as small as one cares to make it. The parson may be the only man of standing in the village and he is expected to take an interest in many things besides his church. Visiting will almost certainly be done on foot even to a farm a mile or two away, because of all the contacts made en route. The Young Farmers' Club is one of the key organizations and, if there is one, steps can be taken to introduce the agricultural occasions of Plough Sunday, Rogation and Lammas, in addition to the ubiquitous Harvest Festival. They are very picturesque and full of meaning.

Only a tiny handful may come to church and there may be very few people who are willing to do anything; a treasurer may be hard to find; few people are willing to accept responsibility. A further snag is that if one upsets one villager, this may involve upsetting all his relations; and that may be quite a percentage of the population.

(b) The Country Town

Bishops know that these are perhaps the most eagerly sought after appointments in the Church of England. Often there is a magnificent church and it is probably the only one in the town; congregations are large and financial problems few. The incumbent is a very important member of the local community and no town meeting, indeed no town occasion, is complete without him. In these days of curate shortage he may well be on his own and his job may become very demanding and very exhausting.

(c) The Urban Working-class Parish

There must be many such. I told the story of one of them in my *The Parish Seeks the Way* (Mowbray, 1962). Many of them are just heart-breaking, for nobody comes to church, nobody seems to care and there is apparently little the parish priest can do about it. There *are* working-class parishes where people go to church in good numbers especially in the North; they can certainly be found in Bristol. But there are areas where people just do not go to church: East London appears to be one and some of the South Bank areas in the Southwark diocese are others. I believe there are some parish churches where the numbers attending any service can be counted on the fingers of two hands. The case for not appointing any incumbent to full-time service in such parishes is overwhelming. Diocesan bishops must be gravely concerned about the plight of the incumbent in the parish where only a few come to church and where there is no sign that even an absolutely brilliant man full of energy, skill and ideas could make any discernible difference.

(d) The Urban Middle-class Parish

These parishes are the backbone of the Church of England, the parishes where people really care and come to church, often in very large numbers. In these parishes everything seems to go well. In addition to flourishing congregations you get lively youth clubs, strong Mothers' Union branches, excellent choirs and Sunday schools that are models of their kind. These are the parishes that are strong supporters of the various missionary societies and indeed of every good cause. Of course there can be troubles and difficulties. Satan is always most active in the parishes where things are going well. Perhaps the chief danger is that one can become complacement and self-satisfied, refusing to see that there is anything very much wrong with the Church of England and wanting to continue old patterns rather than make any changes.

(e) The City Centre Parish

These parishes often have small populations because they include the High Street and shops that were once owner-occupied are now company owned. The parish church may be a cathedral-like building and all the other parishes in the town may have been carved out of it. Congregations may continue to be very large. People may come in from considerable distances, often because of childhood loyalties or a sentimental attachment. The choir and ringers are often superlatively good and for that reason members of other churches may like to come now and again. The incumbent is likely to be a very busy man: he may be mayor's chaplain and have considerable civic responsibilities; he will certainly become heavily involved in diocesan affairs; he may be rural dean; he may be a Proctor in Convocation; he will get many invitations to every conceivable function and if he does not learn to say 'no' occasionally he will soon wear himself out; he will also have to entertain and to make considerable demands on his wife.

In city centres there are sometimes large numbers of parish churches and it is difficult to find a suitable use for them. The residents have moved away. In the City of London most of the remaining city churches are designated as Guild churches and each one fulfils a specialized role and is spared the necessity of having Sunday services that nobody attends. Many of them have lunch-hour services on weekdays, with musical recitals and lectures and demonstrations of all kinds. In Bristol and Norwich a number of interesting uses have been found for city churches no longer required for public worship. Obviously fine medieval buildings of historic interest cannot possibly be demolished.

(f) The New Housing Area

Perhaps this is the most challenging of all parish assignments. There may be thousands of new houses, and almost no church life at all. At weekends some people are too busy with their new gardens and their new houses to bother about church or perhaps they drive into the nearby town to spend the day with their relations.

There may be several hundred baptisms during the year and thousands of forms to sign. There will be vast areas of welfare work, with marriage breakdown problems, drug addiction, promiscuity and violence. The incumbent will certainly have to work very closely with the various social and welfare workers. Just about every known denomination makes a determined onslaught on the new housing area: Pentecostalists, Seventh Day Adventists, Elim Four Square and many others. The better known ones will all be there too: Roman Catholic, Methodist, United Reformed, Baptist, Salvation Army. It is by no means unknown for all the clergy concerned to combine to form a united ministry, with two or more denominations sharing a church building. No man should be left in such a demanding and soul-destroying situation for longer than, say, five years.

(g) The Ethnic Minority Parish

There are now very many parishes in big towns such as London, Bristol, Liverpool, Leicester and Bradford where substantial numbers of West Africans, West Indians, Pakistanis, etc. are to be found. The problems posed for the incumbent are often substantial. Very often the people concerned are Moslems, Sikhs or Hindus who resolutely maintain their own separate identity and their own places of worship. Those who came as Christians may soon have become disenchanted with what they found and especially with services that strike them as being cold and formal. Some Anglican churches are succeeding marvellously in bridging cultural gaps and introducing the very kind of liveliness that is such a popular feature in some of the churches back home. Integration has taken place. There is no apartheid. A wonderful job is being done by some of the clergy in some areas where riots used to take place but do not occur now. It is amazing what the right hand extended in genuine friendship can do to people who feel that their colour makes them unwelcome here.

(8) *Job Prospects*

The Church of England owes a debt of gratitude to Colin
Buchanan for his painstaking survey of the available facts
and figures in his *The Job Prospects of the Anglican Clergy*
(Grove Books, 1972). It is a formidable survey and his
conclusions appear to be indisputable. There is no shortage of
clergy for the available incumbency jobs now and there is no
need for despondency about job prospects in the future. He
says:

> None of the above suggests that the actual *ministry* of the Church
> of England needs to be run down, whether "ministry" is seen in
> terms of the men or the function they fulfil. It only relates to full-
> time jobs. The Church of England will have to travel much lighter
> in its financial, employment and institutional features in the years
> ahead. But that does not mean it need languish. (Page 24)

It certainly need not languish. The job of the parish priest
is still as rewarding and as demanding as ever. The
population of England is roughly forty-six million and of
these roughly twenty-six million are baptized members of the
Church of England. Most of them do not go to church but
most of them strongly insist that they belong. They still want
their babies baptized; nearly half of all marriages take place
in our parish churches. We have opportunities on every side.
We are warmly welcomed when we visit people in nine
homes out of ten. People who do come to church, and people
who do not, want our help and advice when grave trouble
and especially bereavement comes into the family. In a
village the parson really is the *persona* if he identifies himself
with the various sides of village life. In the town his
opportunities for doing good are limitless and his opportunities for preaching the gospel are by no means
insignificant.

What Colin Buchanan has to say does not date with the
passing of the years. Years after it was written it is still right
up-to-date and I suspect it will be well into the nineties. The
Church of England is going to have to continue to watch

carefully those financial, employment and institutional features he mentions (it always ought to have done), but it is certainly not going to languish. Young men of good educational attainments and sure faith should still be encouraged to offer for what most of us regard as the most worthwhile of all jobs. We are concerned with people all the time and there is no dreary sameness.

Chapter 2

The Parish Priest

(1) *The Job*

'Daddy, what is that man for?' If Daddy is a dedicated and informed Christian he might say something like this: 'That man is meant to be a channel for the love of God. He may not be a particularly good man or even an outstandingly clever one but all the same he has been chosen by God and commissioned by the Church for this work. You want to know what he is meant to do? His job is to pray and to lead others to pray, to make Christians and to show the whole parish something of the love of God.' In this chapter I want to look at the man and the job; and I must not give the impression that the parish priest must be a superman, a master of every craft and a model of smooth and poised efficiency.

(2) *Theological Colleges*

Every parson has to be trained. Normally this would involve residence at a theological college but there are no absolute and invariable rules. Graduates in theology are expected to do two years if they are under 25, and non-graduates a four-year degree and ordination training course at one of the colleges that provide such a course. Graduates aged 25–29 would spend three years and those aged 30–39 two years full-

time training. Candidates aged 40 and over spend up to two
years or whatever period their bishop requires. Candidates
aged 30 or over for stipendiary ministry may now choose
whether to train for two years full-time at college or for three
years part-time on a regional theological course. Full details
can be found in the current edition of *Theological Training in
the Church of England* (ACCM publication). There is such
insistence on high standards that every theological college is
in a university area, and the university links are becoming
closer and closer.

Here is a list of present theological colleges, with the
relevant university link and the number of places (1984
figures).

Theological College	University	Number of Places
The Queen's College, Birmingham (Interdenominational)	Birmingham	37
Trinity College, Bristol	CNAA	72
Ridley Hall, Cambridge	Cambridge	50
Westcott House, Cambridge (Ridley and Westcott together with Wesley House and Westminster College form the Cambridge Federation of Theological Colleges)	Cambridge	47
Chichester	Southampton	52
Ripon College, Cuddesdon	Oxford	70
Cranmer Hall, Durham	Durham	77
Lincoln	Nottingham/Hull	70
Oak Hill	CNAA	68
Mirfield	Leeds	40
St John's, Nottingham	Nottingham	98
St Stephen's House, Oxford	Oxford	58
Wycliffe Hall, Oxford	Oxford	67
Salisbury and Wells	Southampton	72
Total number of places		878

Part-Time Courses	University	Dioceses mainly served
Canterbury School of Ministry		Canterbury and Carlisle
Carlisle Diocesan Training Institute		Carlisle
East Anglian Ministerial Training Course		Ely, Norwich, St Edmundsbury and Ipswich
East Midlands Ministry Training Course	Nottingham	Derby, Leicester, Lincoln, Southwell
Exeter/Truro Non-stipendiary Ministry Scheme	Exeter	Exeter, Truro
Gloucester School for Ministry		Gloucester and Hereford
Oak Hill Non-stipendiary Ministry Course		Chelmsford, St Albans, London
Southwark Ordination Course	London	Guildford, London, Southwark, Rochester
North East Ordination Course		Durham, Newcastle, York
Northern Ordination Course		Blackburn, Bradford, Chester, Liverpool, Manchester, Ripon, Sheffield, Wakefield, York
Oxford Diocesan Non-stipendiary Ministry Scheme		Oxford
St Albans Diocese Ministerial Training Scheme		St Albans
Southern Dioceses Ministerial Training Scheme		Bath and Wells, Chichester, Portsmouth, Salisbury, Winchester
West Midlands Ministerial Training Course		Birmingham, Worcester, Lichfield, Coventry

Other Colleges and Courses

Edinburgh Theological College	Edinburgh
St Michael's, Llandaff	University of Wales
St Deiniol's Library, Hawarden	

Pre-Theological College: The Aston Training Scheme

Many candidates for ordination who are under twenty-five do not have the necessary five passes in academic subjects in GCE and two at A level. These (and any candidate under 35) may be required to undertake the Aston Training Scheme prior to beginning training at theological college. This scheme replaced Ian Ramsey College, Brasted, and it is intended to help candidates who have few educational qualifications to develop academic confidence, to widen their knowledge of the Christian life and to deepen their self understanding before they begin formal training for ordination (or professional lay ministry). The course is part-time and lasts two years.

Women preparing to be deaconesses or serve as professional lay ministers now attend selection conferences and undertake the same training as ordinands. It should be noted that the Deacons (Ordination of Women) Measure is at present passing through the General Synod.

I know from some personal experience that the part-time non-stipendiary ministry courses really do provide excellent training but the need for residential theological colleges does not diminish.

Academic training is by no means the only or even the most important side of theological college life. Men are taught to adopt disciplined habits of prayer, study and service to the community. They are taught to think theologically. They are expected to question and to examine. The hope is that they will end their course with a mature and definite faith in the love of God and his good purposes fulfilled in the person of Jesus. If they have not been to a university (and somewhere around 50 per cent of all ordinands are non-graduates) they will learn how to live in community, how to appreciate the other man's point of view, how to differ without acrimony from somebody whose whole outlook may be very different from their own.

But the system, of course, has its limitations. It could be that few of the staff have had long and close experience of parish work. It could be that ideas of what being a parish priest really involves are strangely deficient, often indeed completely false. Quite a few ordinands seem to think that nearly all parish churches are sparsely attended by an assortment of people who are chiefly female and all elderly, that they are thoroughly run down and desperately short of money and that the wretched incumbents are, to a man, depressed and pessimistic about the future. These men are likely to be in for a pleasant surprise if they take the choosing of a first curacy very seriously.

(3) *The First Curacy*

It is a man's first curacy that is of great importance. It is usual for a parish priest who needs a curate to write fully to one or more theological colleges. The principal can put all these letters together in a file for the ordinands to read for themselves or he can make up a short-list for each man.

The demand for curates greatly exceeds the supply. The applicant must first of all satisfy himself that the church in the parish really is alive, that people really come to it in quite large numbers, that there really are people to whom he can minister. Men are sometimes mistakenly advised for their first curacy to go to tough districts where perhaps the incumbent has an impossible task: he is run off his feet, with tens of thousands of parishioners, a couple of day schools, two or three large hospitals and perhaps a prison; few people come to church though the incumbent works for sixteen hours a day. It may be praiseworthy for a curate to want to go to such a parish but it ought to be discouraged because that man may well break his heart. He should choose a parish where the church really counts for something in the local community.

It is also of paramount importance that the training incumbent should be somebody with whom the man feels *en rapport*. His first vicar can make him or mar him. There are one or two points that the ordinand should carefully note. Is the church clean and tidy, with notice-boards bearing signs of recent attention? Is the vicarage study a place of order or chaos? Does the vicar offer to pay expenses of travel; and was his wife, if he has one, invited to come along as well? Is the vicar keen and enthusiastic or rather dreary and depressed? Has he a sense of humour? Does he believe in delegating or does he seem to be the type that wants to do everything himself? Does he volunteer any information about a rough daily schedule of work, salary and allowances, holidays, weekly day off, and daily time spent with the family? If he is too spiritually minded to think such comparatively minor matters worthy of attention, then be on guard!

Normally a man will spend a minimum of three years in his first curacy. It is likely to be five years or so before he becomes an incumbent or priest-in-charge. So a second curacy is desirable in order to gain additional experience. A man may well be much less selfish in his choice of a second curacy and he may agree to go where those in authority think it best for him. His second curacy could be in a really tough area where people do not seem to care but where there is good reason to suppose that the people are going to respond.

(4) *The First Living*

How does a man get appointed to his first living or get his first appointment as priest-in-charge? It may well be that the bishop will approach him and ask him to go to one that he considers suitable, or it may be that a private patron or patronage society will offer him something. Until recently it was thought unethical to approach anybody to ask for a job but this, happily, is no longer the case. Vacant livings are often advertised in the *Church Times*, and there is a Clergy Appointments Adviser whose job it is to help priests returning from abroad or resident in England to find suitable new appointments. He also helps patrons to find the right man and produces regularly a list of vacant benefices.

The patron, even if he is the bishop, does not have the only say. The PCC makes representations when there is a vacancy and the churchwardens commonly interview anybody whom the patron thinks suitable. Everything possible is done to ensure that the right man goes to the right job and that he can and will work with the people in the parish.

Under section 67 of the Pastoral Measure 1983 the bishop may, with the consent of the pastoral committee and after consultation with the patron and PCC, decide that for a period of no more than five years no presentation may be made. He may appoint instead a priest-in-charge. This device is often used when the whole future of the benefice is under consideration (perhaps it is the subject of a pastoral scheme). The priest-in-charge is, for all practical purposes, the incumbent, but he has no freehold and the bishop may withdraw his licence when he thinks he has been there long enough. There is no objection to a man being licensed as priest-in-charge of several benefices nor to an incumbent being so appointed to another benefice.

The applicant should investigate the material side of things before accepting anything. He is foolish indeed if he does not, because it is unlikely that subsequent opportunities will occur for him to get changes made. He must see what the house is like in terms of upkeep, for his wife will almost certainly have to work it alone without domestic help and he will have to manage the garden and the boiler. In spite of so much being done, there are still hopelessly large, cold and expensive parsonage houses around, and PCCs that insist on such houses being retained are doing future incumbents a disservice. A new incumbent ought to be provided with a comfortable, easily managed house that is adequate for his needs and possible for his pocket.

What do you do if it gradually becomes clear that you are not in the right parish? It does happen. Remember that John Wesley was very far from successful in East Anglia but achieved astonishing results in Bristol and in Cornwall. The right course is to consult the bishop. Diocesan bishops welcome free and frank discussion with an incumbent and will almost certainly have helpful suggestions to make. Some of them post a list of all diocesan vacancies in the diocesan office.

Perhaps the best way of all of obtaining a new appointment is to get in touch with the Clergy Appointments Adviser. He is appointed by the Archbishops of Canterbury and York for this very purpose. His address is Fielden House, Little College Street, London SW1P 3SH (tel. 01-222-9544/5). It is also possible to get one's name on the Lord Chancellor's list by writing to the Secretary for Church Appointments, 10 Downing Street, London SW1. He will want references.

(5) *The Priorities*

In studying priorities it may be useful to glance at a 'Top Twenty' list I drew up to help deacons to sort out which things are of most importance and which things of lesser importance.

1. **Taking Services.** Obviously this must be placed high on the list. It includes Sunday and weekday services.
2. **Evangelism.** Attempting to make converts, seeking to get in touch with those outside the worshipping fellowship.
3. **Personal Prayer Life.** Studying the Bible, reading other books, meditation, self-examination, the practice of the presence of God.

4. **Support for the Church Overseas.** Taking this seriously, encouraging informed prayer support and financial support and understanding of the problems confronting those working overseas.

5. **Personal Righteousness of Worshipping Members.** Seeing that faith involves behaviour, not hesitating to rebuke sin regardless of persons or consequences (see rubric before 1662 Holy Communion service). It is not easy to list this duty under some simple heading but it is certainly one imposed upon us at ordination.

6. **Ecumenical Activities.** Looking for ways of co-operating with members of other denominations, seeking to understand what they stand for, trying to see the problem theologically.

7. **Preaching and Teaching.** Sermon preparation, expounding the Scriptures, building up knowledge of the faith by all available methods both in church and outside it.

8. **Visiting the Sick and the Whole.** Calling on people in their homes and hospital, pastoral visiting; the ministry of healing and the ministry of penance might be considered here.

9. **Rest.** Adequate rest, weekly day off, recreation, hobbies, family life, annual holiday.

10. **Seeking and Training Leaders.** Looking out for people able and willing to take responsibility in leading organizations, for holding office, for all money matters, for social events, for helping in just about everything. Training these leaders.

11. **Encouraging Vocations.** Looking out for ordinands from all age groups, as well as missionary recruits and potential readers. Encouraging young people to go in for careers involving service to the community.

12. **Welfare Work.** Getting to know the workings of the welfare state and the officers responsible for running it, becoming involved with Samaritans and local humanitarian organizations of all kinds, helping people in

trouble (whether churchgoers or not), being part of the caring Church.

13. **Desk Work.** Writing letters, editing the magazine, preparing circular letters, choosing hymns, working out special services, looking up or drawing up special prayers, filling in forms, keeping a filing system.

14. **Christian Initiation.** Preparation and instruction of parents and godparents for the public ministration of Holy Baptism, seeking out and preparing confirmation candidates, caring for them afterwards.

15. **Christian Marriage.** Personal interviews, personal preparation, group preparation, rehearsal of the ceremony, helping when things go wrong.

16. **Committee Work Inside the Parish.** Meetings of the PCC, finance committee, management committees, school managers, meetings of organizations, sub-committees.

17. **Committee Work Outside the Parish.** Diocesan committees, society committees, London committees, local committees of all kinds.

18. **Church Fabric.** Keeping a vigilant eye on the fabric of all church buildings, paying attention to boilers, roofs, drains, water courses, churchyards, beautifying and improving as opportunity offers, preparing the church for Sunday and other services.

19. **Youth Work.** Involvement with youth organizations of all kinds, trying to understand the point of view of the beat generation, leading young people to full commitment, taking an interest in youth organizations not connected with the church.

20. **Being Neighbourly with Nearby Anglican Churches.** Seeing whether a group or team ministry is possible, helping in other parishes when called upon, getting to know neighbouring Anglicans at least as well as neighbouring Nonconformists.

On many occasions I have handed out duplicated copies of

this list to PCCs, chapter meetings, deanery synods and youth conferences, divided those present into groups and asked each group to decide which they considered to be the three most important jobs and the three least important ones. The groups have usually consisted of committed Christians and in most of them Taking Services and Personal Prayer Life have been in the top three. Committee Work Inside the Parish and Committee Work Outside the Parish are almost always in the bottom three. Visiting the Sick and The Whole is always well up and so is Preaching and Teaching. Desk Work, curiously, is generally very low down on the list.

(6) *Sermons*

The incumbent regards work in his study as of very great importance and it is there that he will do, amongst other things, his sermon preparation. Preb. Cleverley Ford and the College of Preachers have surely done much to restore the general idea of the importance of the sermon, and literature can be obtained from the College of Preachers, St Margaret Pattens Church, Eastcheap, London EC3M 1HS. B. K. Cunningham at Westcott House used to tell his men to keep two books going all the time, one serious theological work and one lighter one, and to use both as sermon material. A man who does not keep up his theological reading will find himself with nothing worthwhile to say by the time he has reached the age of forty.

A sensible method is to start to think about the Sunday sermon or sermons on Tuesdays and gradually jot down ideas and illustrations, writing the sermon out in full on Fridays. On Saturday mornings the intercessions and notices can be written out and on Saturday nights the sermon can be learned. Some will learn by heart, some will content themselves with a list of headings. If the vicar reads his sermon and it looks and sounds as though it is being read, it will make far less impact than one that is preached, with the preacher looking at the congregation and sensing whether he is holding their attention or not. Every sermon ought to be written out in full. The biggest menace in the pulpit is the preacher who gets there without having prepared anything and who depends upon the inspiration of the moment. The sermon really matters: it is essential that it should be heard and it should be understood. The beginning is vitally important: in the first minute or so you have caught the attention of the congregation or lost it and, if you have lost it, it is hard indeed to regain.

What do you do with old sermons? Some burn them; some keep them for say ten years; some, including the writer, have all the sermons they have ever preached carefully filed and indexed and immediately accessible. My system has the merit of extreme simplicity. I have an ordinary foolscap filing cabinet. The top drawer did very well to start with but before long I needed more. Every Sunday in the Church's year has its own file and so do all the regular special occasions, the major saints' days and the occasional special services. There are files for Mayor's Sunday, Remembrance Sunday, the Week of Prayer for Christian Unity, Hospital Sunday, Weddings, Funerals, Schools' services, Mothers' Union, Overseas Missions, Home Missions, Stewardship Sunday, United Nations Sunday, Holiday sermons and a growing list of Lent courses.

Probably one brand-new sermon will be prepared every Sunday. Few parsons are really capable of producing more than one new and properly prepared sermon each week. For the rest, suitable old ones can be rewritten and brought up to date and used again. An old one must *never* be extracted late on Saturday evening and made to do duty just as it is.

On the inside cover of each file each sermon in that file is listed under its number and subject. A separate indexed notebook is kept with a page or several pages for every book in the Bible and the texts are entered with the number of the file containing a sermon on that text. By this means it is possible to turn to a sermon on any text you have ever used.

You write on top of each sermon the church in which it was preached and the date and perhaps a note about how it went. You generally know which sermon really made an impact and which did not and it is a salutary discipline to make a note. Further comments on sermons will be found in Chapter 8.

After each festival or special occasion notes can be made and slipped in the file listing all the points that seem worth attention: numbers of communicants perhaps, details about the ceremonial or music, things that were not done well and things that could be done differently. It is a great help when, say, Remembrance Sunday comes round to see where things went wrong last time. A mistake made once can be excused but not when the same mistake is made time after time. Any leaflets or posters can also be conveniently stored in the sermon file and so can any ideas or comments or illustrations that might be useful later on.

(7) *The Filing System*

Every incumbent receives a minor avalanche of correspondence and literature. If you have secretarial help it is quite easy. But even if you have none, letters must be answered as quickly as possible. If you can type it makes the keeping of copies so much easier. What do you do with the copies so that they can be referred to without waste of time? Perhaps this is the moment to look at the equipment that every parson's study should have.

On my desk I used to have a 'desk secretary' that I found invaluable. It contained expanding pockets divided into (1) days of the month, for filing papers for forward attention and all papers relating to future engagements, (2) months of the year for future action papers, and (3) an alphabetical section for facts, figures, sermon illustrations you may want later on, and so on. I doubt whether these useful things can be bought now but it is a simple matter to adapt one or perhaps two indexed box files for all the purposes described. This arrangement will not look as tidy on your desk but it will be a great deal cheaper.

To have everything right in front of you on your desk is most helpful. There should also be a desk diary which should be most carefully filled in whenever new entries in your pocket diary are made. By this means your wife can tell at a glance if you are or are not available when somebody calls or phones when you are out. You are also safeguarded if by some mischance you mislay your pocket diary. Also on your desk you will need a basket for work waiting and one of those with three trays is probably the best. Then the top one can contain immediate items, the next one less urgent items and the bottom one the least urgent items of all.

One of your bookcases should be within easy reach of the desk because it will contain the books that have to be referred to daily and perhaps several times a day—different versions of the Bible, commentaries, reference books of all kinds, copies of the parish magazine, books of prayers, the hymn book. A most useful item of equipment is a cabinet containing many drawers of what used to be foolscap size. Nowadays the size is A4, between foolscap and quarto; half of A4 is called A5 and half of that again is A6. Obviously the time is coming when foolscap and quarto sizes are unobtainable but the old foolscap cabinets will serve very adequately indefinitely. Each drawer can be labelled—banns application forms, baptism forms, book and other catalogues, personal bills, parish magazine matter, churchwardens' items, treasurer's items, newspaper cuttings and special forms of service of all kinds. But none of these is a substitute for a four-drawer filing cabinet. The top drawer can be marked 'sermons', the next one 'parish', the third 'diocese, etc.', and the bottom one perhaps 'personal'. Each drawer will contain many separate files that are alphabetically arranged and as some of the matters filed will certainly be confidential it is as well to have a cabinet that can be locked.

Matters sent by the bishop should be carefully filed, for it is important to know what the bishop's ruling is on certain matters and he does not want all his incumbents writing or phoning for his views on matters that have already been committed to writing. Letters from the diocesan secretary and the board of finance will need special folders. Benefice statistics have to be carefully prepared and sent to Church House at intervals and it is a help if they are all kept in one folder and brought up to date annually. Letters on various matters should be kept in order of date and soon some pretty bulky files will take shape. It really is astonishing just how much paper is required in the running of the average parish.

(8) *Visiting*

Visiting also requires much paper work. The parish priest must visit his people and not listen to those who say visiting is a waste of time as people are never in. This is nonsense: in many areas less than half of the women have full-time jobs. As you do your rounds you find women at home, menfolk at home on holiday or off sick, large numbers of elderly retired people and perhaps quite a few lonely housebound ones.

A sad feature of many a town (and many a village) is that you are likely to find at home some of those who, through no fault of their own, are unemployed. They may be bored, frustrated and angry with a system that seems unable to find a place for them. They may well be delighted to see the parson taking a personal interest in them, and not only to work off steam. Who was it who said that man's extremity is God's opportunity? Five good visits per afternoon is a reasonable target.

Visiting has several objects: you should get to know your people and be seen to be taking an interest in their spiritual lives, to find out if they have any problems or worries, and to help in any way possible. What you must not do is just get inside somebody's home and wait to be entertained, compelling the unfortunate hostess to think out the small talk. Such visiting does more harm than good and, if the parson has this sort of reputation, he will find many doors will remain closed to him.

Visiting needs to be methodical. You should have an indexed notebook with every street listed under the appropriate letter; it should be pocket sized and so easily carried. On arrival home it is sound practice to enter the name of each person visited on a card which fits into a card index cabinet of which there are several patterns. The circular kind is quickest for turning up the right card in a moment but it costs perhaps £60. The Myers Rondofile contains 1,000 cards with divisions A to Z and is surely admirable for those who can afford this sort of thing. The old fashioned small card-index cabinet complete with cards and A to Z divisions costs perhaps £5 and I always found this perfectly adequate. My last one lasted sixteen years! The size card had better be A6, providing ample space for all necessary entries.

On each card you enter the name, address and phone number, if any, and then list the information you have managed to jot down during the visit—names and ages of children, husband's occupation, whether confirmed, which services are normally attended, membership of organizations and date of visit. A large notebook can be kept in your desk which contains lists of names of people to visit with addresses and this list is constantly being added to. New names are collected perhaps after Sunday service as you stand at the church door for the chief purpose of making the acquaintance of newcomers. There will also be people with various troubles, cases of sickness, loss of job, the marriage breaking up, the son getting into bad ways, trouble with the police and so on. Some names may be given to you by others, for instance the probation officer or the hospital chaplain or another incumbent.

(9) *Daily Prayers*

One's day begins with the daily office in church, with Holy Communion following either daily or at least on major saints' days. Often the office has to be said alone. Some priests always follow it with their personal prayers and many of us have done this for so many years that any plan which left them out would seem strangely deficient. A good scheme for morning prayer is the old five finger exercise, the first standing for members of our own families, the second for the parish and other people generally, the middle finger for those in high places, the fourth for the weak and troubled and the fifth, the little one, for oneself. The ASB Morning and Evening Prayer provide plenty of time after the lessons for the quiet meditation which is so important. Those who say the daily offices alone may find *Psalms from Taize* (Mowbray) an inspiration but if others attend it is best to stick to the ASB wording.

There will be people for whom the parish priest prays by name but not everybody finds it helpful to have immensely long lists of names each day—those being prepared for marriage, those being baptized, those preparing for confirmation, those visited the previous day, those who are going to be visited and so on. But it certainly is important to pray by name for the weak and frail and for those in trouble.

(10) *Desk Work*

Perhaps the daily offices are at 7.45 a.m. or thereabouts. In that case you get home for breakfast at say 8.45 a.m. and you are in your study soon after 9 a.m. The letters have to be read and after that perhaps you will want to spend a short while glancing at the daily newspaper. The temptation to spend the next hour reading it is one to be resisted and this temptation is particularly strong on *Church Times* or *Church of England Newspaper* mornings. By 9.30 a.m. one should be seated at one's desk getting down to the task of letter answering and desk work generally.

The ideal is to stay at one's desk until lunch but this is hardly ever possible. Callers will come. There may be mid-morning celebrations of Holy Communion, funerals, meetings of all kinds, private communions and urgent sick calls. After lunch a short rest may well be taken with a more leisurely look at the daily paper and then out one goes to visit until Evensong. Said Evensong may well be timed for 5 p.m. so that you get home soon after 5.30 p.m. in time for the high tea which is the most sensible arrangement in a vicarage. What time off does a man have for his family? It should be at least two hours daily and during this time parishioners should be urged to leave you alone. Every parson ought to have a certain minimum of time with his wife and family without parish responsibilities.

(11) *The Incumbent's Wife*

What part does the incumbent's wife play? It should be made clear that although PCCs without exception ask for a married man they certainly do not expect or even want the parson's wife to be an unpaid curate. It is clearly understood that her first duty is to her home, her husband and her children. From harsh economic necessity many a parson's wife now goes out to work, but it is not because she does not have enough to do or because she is bored at home. A parson's wife has a fascinating job, if she cares to become involved. In a short space of time she is known and accepted and many problems and queries are brought to her. She can take a leading part in many organizations; enrolling members of the Mothers' Union is only one of several possibilities. But she must certainly not do many things that other women can perfectly well do. It is a great mistake for her to do all the flower arranging or to act as organist, even if she does either of these duties supremely well and others lack her skills. They can be trained and they can improve; doing a job for the church is a wonderful thing for deepening commitment and keeping interest.

The parson's wife will know many of the parish secrets because they will be communicated to her direct by the persons concerned but she must never ask her husband to disclose confidential matters because she knows that his discretion must be absolute. It is disquieting to find that so many people think that confidential matters are freely bandied around in the vicarage by the one person who should be known to be completely and utterly discreet.

(12) *Evening Work*

After the mid-evening spell with one's family there will almost certainly be evening engagements—looking in at choir practice and bell ringing, looking in at the various organizations, attending meetings of the PCC, finance committee, house groups, confirmation classes, deanery or diocesan affairs, civic matters, meetings of various church societies, charities and good causes generally. The difficulty is fitting in all that one wants to do. Some time has to be found for evening visits but they must not clash with favourite television programmes.

It is also a good idea to keep one evening free and to make it known that callers can come to the vicarage without appointment. If it is made public that the vicar will be home from 7.30 p.m. to 9.30 p.m. to see anybody about anything he may well have a surprise. It is amazing what a variety of callers there will probably be, varying from requests to sign forms to something really deep. It ought to be better known that one of the canons of the Church of England, C24 section 6, runs: '. . . and he shall provide opportunities whereby any of his parishioners may resort unto him for spiritual counsel and advice'.

(13) *Time Off*

Some time off daily is important. One day a week off is equally so and your people should be told what day it is and should be asked to leave you alone unless something really important arises. Regular holidays are important too. Some parishes give all the clergy the inside of a week off after

Christmas (Sunday night to the following Friday night), the outside of a week off after Easter (Sunday night until the following Friday week) and nearly a month off in the summer including three Sundays. It ought to be possible to cover weekday services and weekday duties easily enough by mutual arrangements with a neighbour. Sunday services are more difficult but again arrangements can usually be made even if services have to be fewer in number than usual.

There may well be a retired cleric or two in the vicinity. Remember, most of them are delighted to be asked to celebrate (this most of all), preach, take a funeral or wedding or pay a visit in the sort of emergencies that so often crop up when one is away. The retired man will of course receive the appropriate wedding or funeral fee. Most dioceses lay down a scale of fees and expenses for Sunday duty taken by a retired man and it is right to offer them. Some parishes are in no state financially to offer anything; many retired clerics will gladly help out in such circumstances without receiving a penny in fees and regard it as a privilege to be asked to do so.

As we work pretty long hours, not far short of a sixty-hour week on average, these breaks are all the more important. I am never really very impressed by the man who boasts that he has not had a day off for twenty years and I cannot help wondering whether such a man really has many days on. If the Almighty needed one day of rest in seven it seems presumptuous to suppose that we can manage with less.

(14) *Further Commitments*

The parish must come first in any scheme of priorities. But there will surely be other commitments and it is quite wrong to neglect the parish in favour of things that may seem to be more glamorous and more exciting. As one becomes more senior these will steadily increase because our whole system of working is geared to the idea of voluntary effort. It is true that some work will be paid but we do not keep the pay. It is taken into account when working out the stipend augmentation. The sort of things we can expect to be asked to do are these: hospital chaplaincies, other chaplaincies such as Sea Cadets, mayor's chaplain, Actors' Church Union chaplain, service on diocesan committees, service on church society committees or charity committees, becoming a member of the Cathedral chapter or perhaps being elected a Proctor in Convocation.

There may well be many non-church commitments. Some incumbents find it very useful to be elected to the parish council or to the district council or even to the county council. There is much to be gained from joining cultural associations of every kind, organizations which exist to preserve amenities, improve the environment or deepen knowledge. Willingness to serve as a school governor should be made known. Service on the area health authority may be possible. Many incumbents find that membership of the local Rotary Club, Lions or Round Table provides valuable contacts as well as a useful field of service.

(15) *The Staff Meeting*

There is one other job that is vitally important, challenging and demanding: training assistant curates. Usually the bishop decides that some parishes in his diocese are to be training parishes and this decision is made perhaps because of the nature of the parish or perhaps because of the calibre of the incumbent. Such a parish can expect a steady flow of deacons. Training them is fascinating. In this case, a weekly staff meeting is imperative. Some hold it on Mondays or Tuesdays when the bias is towards holding an inquest on the previous Sunday's services. Some prefer Saturday, for then the bias is quite definitely towards the following day. At a Saturday meeting the very latest information is available about the sick to be prayed for by name. At the staff meeting the arrangements for the services and all weekday engagements will be carefully made on a duplicated duty list. It is necessary for all the duties for the following two months to be worked out in good time—and if it comes to that, holiday periods should be agreed well in advance. Lists of names will be considered of the sick and housebound and an eye will be kept on the regularity of the visits paid.

Private communions and the names of those in hospital will be considered and visiting lists will be compared and perhaps some case work done. Parish policy will be considered. Our lay members have a right to expect their clergy to think things out in detail before presenting proposals and to give a lead. At times the organist or the churchwardens or the treasurer will be invited to attend. The new deacon and indeed any curate should regard the incumbent as somebody whom they can approach at any time and not a distant over-busy figure who simply has no time for their problems. The incumbent is trying to teach the men their job as parish priests. It should not be assumed that they know the answers to virtually all parish problems just because they have spent several years in a theological college. There they learn the theory. It is with us that they learn how to put theory into practice. Those of us who have curates are the fortunate ones; we can learn from them of fresh ideas and new approaches.

Obviously in a parish where there is one or more non-stipendiary assistant clergy the staff meeting must be held on Saturdays if they are ever going to attend. Remembering that Saturdays really belong to their families it might be reasonable to invite them to attend say once a month or when there is something they ought to know about and when their opinions ought to be heard. Where the clergy, whether full-time or non-stipendiary, are unmarried, it is an excellent custom to have them to lunch afterwards.

The parish priest will end his day on his knees and his night prayers may well be based on Adoration, Contrition and Thanksgiving. He will surely have much to confess in his daily act of self-examination. He will most certainly have a very great deal for which he will want to render humble and hearty thanks.

38   *A Handbook of Parish Work*

(16) *The Ordination of Women to the Priesthood*

I have written this chapter on the assumption that the parish priest will always be a man. But will this always be so? Some of us devoutly hope that it will not. The General Synod has decided that there are no theological objections to women being ordained priests and has decided that they may be ordained deacons.

For all too long our Church of England has treated women, who form the bulk of our congregations, very badly. There are still those who want to see women doing only such things as providing refreshments, cleaning and polishing, taking round the magazine and arranging the flowers, while men do the most important things. This is extraordinary when you consider that in every other profession women are treated as equals and fill the top posts with competence and dignity.

The objectors generally tend to belong to the extreme wings of our Church. Conservative Evangelicals claim that the Bible forbids women even to speak in church. Anglo-Catholics hold that as Rome does not ordain women it must be wrong. I well remember that debate in General Synod when it was decided there were no theological objections, when the late Professor Geoffrey Lampe made mincemeat of all the objections put forward and carried the day. We are rapidly putting ourselves into an impossible position. Various member Churches of the Anglican Communion— for instance, the United States, Canada, Australia and New Zealand—have them. I find it surprising that the argument is put forward that Rome might object if we accepted them, since Rome does not accept the validity of our orders and regards its links with the Free Churches as being as close as those with us. All those who take an immense pride in their membership of the great world-wide Anglican Communion would do well to accept the position as it is; otherwise they may succeed in reducing the historic Catholic Church of this land to no more than a tiny sect.

Chapter 3

Parish Partnership

(1) *The Parish Priest's Authority*

'Send down the Holy Spirit upon your servant N for the office and work of a priest in your Church.' So says the bishop when he ordains. Power and authority are given through the laying on of hands. 'Receive this Book, as a sign of the authority which God has given you this day to preach the gospel of Christ and to minister his Holy Sacraments.' The responsibility is immense.

It goes to some men's heads. They place the emphasis on the *magister* rather than the *minister* role. Smith's Latin Dictionary defines *magister* as 'a master, chief, head, superior, director, president, leader, conductor' while *minister* is 'an inferior, one subject to another, a servant'. A man who sets out to be the *persona* of the parish, the *magister*, can argue that there is reason on his side: at his induction to his benefice the freehold was bestowed upon him and virtually nothing can be done in a parish hall, a church hall, a graveyard or a parsonage house without his express consent. Halsbury's Laws of England (Ecclesiastical Law) states: 'The incumbent is the proper custodian of the keys of the church and of the register books and has a general control over the church including the vestry...' (3rd Edition Vol. 13 para. 314) and no money collected in church can be voted for any purpose without his agreement (3rd Edition Vol. 13

para. 351). It is true that he cannot now do certain things that used to be his prerogative alone. The Canons of the Church of England state for instance that 'no minister shall change the form of vesture in use in the church or chapel in which he officiates unless he has ascertained by consultation with the parochial church council that such changes will be acceptable' (Canon B8). He may not change the forms of service, other than the services known as the occasional offices, in any church in his parish unless the decision to do so 'shall be taken jointly by the minister and the parochial church council' (Canon B3).

(2) *Magister*

But he can still do a great deal without the approval of the PCC or anybody else. For instance, it is clearly stated in Canon B20 that he has supreme authority in matters concerning the music of the church.

1. In all churches and chapels, other than in cathedral or collegiate churches or chapels where the matter is governed by or dependent upon the statutes or customs of the same, it belongs to the minister to direct when the organ shall be played and when it will not be played, and to decide what parts of the service shall be sung.

2. Where there is an organist or choirmaster the minister shall pay due heed to his advice and assistance in the choosing of chants, hymns, anthems, and other settings and in the ordering of the music of the Church; but at all times the final responsibility and decision in these matters rests with the minister.

3. It is the duty of the minister to ensure that only such chants, hymns, anthems, and other settings are chosen as are appropriate, both the words and the music, to the solemn act of worship and prayer in the House of God as well as to the congregation assembled for that purpose; and to banish all irreverence in the practice and in the performance of the same.

It is proposed that Canon B20 should be rewritten so that the hiring and firing is that of the PCC with the concurrence of the incumbent. This is at present at General Approval stage in the Synod.

Canon B35 makes the point even more clear:

> When matrimony is to be solemnised at any church, it belongs to the minister of the parish to decide what music shall be played, what hymns or anthems shall be sung, or what furnishings or flowers should be placed in or about the church for the occasion.

Canon F15 states that the bells are not to be rung at any time 'contrary to the direction of the minister'. In other words, the minister can still utterly wreck the work of the parish and make all the services unendurable if he so desires.

(3) *Minister*

In the great majority of parishes no such breakdown occurs or looks like occurring just because the emphasis is away from *magister* and towards *minister*. Nearly all parish priests remember that they represent the carpenter who humbled himself, taking the form of a servant and girding himself to wash the feet of his disciples. A parish priest comes to a parish to love his people, to work with them in partnership and to share with them and learn from them as well as teach them.

But he will not carry this process too far. He has come to be their servant and not their lackey. He will still be held responsible for whatever happens. If the parish fails to pay its quota or if the church catches fire or is underinsured or if the registers are mislaid or wrongly kept he will certainly be blamed. Equally, if congregations increase, if a tremendous fund-faising effort succeeds magnificently, if the choir wins the choral championship and the dramatic society the challenge cup at the local festival, he will get much of the praise, even though he may not be much of a preacher, useless at money matters, unable to sing a note and incapable of playing the part of the rear half of a pantomime horse.

(4) *The Electoral Roll*

Some maintain that the communicants' roll is the only

worthwhile membership list, for such a roll is a voluntary one. The only compulsory one is the electoral roll, although this is not intended to be a membership list but rather, as the name implies, for election purposes.

Entirely new rolls have to be drawn up every sixth year from 1972. The qualifications for enrolment are (1) baptism (2) membership of the Church of England or another Church of the Anglican Communion or an overseas Church in communion with the Church of England (3) being sixteen years of age or over and (4) being resident in the parish or, if not so resident, habitual attendance at public worship in the parish during a period of six months prior to enrolment.

Oddly enough, a person can be on several electoral rolls if he satisfies the conditions. Every electoral roll should be revised annually. We do not want our electoral rolls to carry dead wood but we do want new members to be on, and preferably lots of them. After all, electoral rolls have come to be regarded as our official membership lists.

(5) *The Annual Parochial Church Meeting*

All on the electoral roll are entitled to attend the annual parochial church meeting. This is the most important meeting of the whole year and must be convened by the incumbent not later than 30 April every year by posting a notice on or near the church door for a period that includes the two Sundays before the meeting. Matters on the agenda should include the reception of a copy of the electoral roll, an annual report on the proceedings of the PCC, a report on the financial affairs of the parish, the audited accounts, a report on the fabric, goods and ornaments of the church or churches, and a report on the proceedings of the deanery synod. The churchwardens are usually elected by the joint action of the incumbent and the parishioners at this meeting, for it has virtually taken the place of the old Easter Vestry meeting. Parochial church councillors are elected but many parishes elect only one third annually. In every third year representatives are elected to the deanery synod. The meeting elects the sidesmen for the year. The incumbent often gives his annual 'state of the parish' message and it is not unusual for the leaders of church organizations to give brief accounts of the year's work.

Quite a good idea, if time is a factor (and it usually is), is to have these brief accounts duplicated and distributed. But leaders should always present them to the meeting with words such as: 'I present the account printed on the paper of the activities of your Junior Youth Club'. It gives the chairman his annual opportunity of saying a public thank you and the meeting can support this with a round of applause.

It matters who the churchwardens are and who serves on the PCC. It is dispiriting for you and for the parish if you have to tout around for people to serve in these crucial capacities, or, even worse, to look around the annual meeting to see if anybody present can be dragooned into service. A far better way is to have a nominations book at the back of the church at least a month before the meeting. There should be space for the names of the proposer and seconder and an indication that the person nominated is willing to serve.

Nominations should be made for churchwarden, membership of the PCC, membership of the deanery synod and sidesmen. The ideal for PCC and deanery synod membership is a ballot, with at least twice as many names as there are vacancies. Ballot papers should be duplicated before the meeting.

Of all these nominations the most important ones are for the two churchwardens. In many a parish one is nominated by the incumbent and the other elected by the meeting, but this is not correct. Both should be elected by the 'joint consent of the minister of the parish and a meeting of the parishioners . . .' according to the Churchwardens (Appointment and Resignation) Measure 1964. It is only if no agreement can be reached that the minister chooses one and the meeting another. Never in my whole ministry have I known this to happen. Relations in a parish must be deplorable if this escape clause has to be employed. There is much to be said for churchwardens continuing in office for (say) a period of three years only; by this means one avoids the difficult situation of an old man who, thinking himself indispensable, expects to be re-elected year after year. There is another great advantage of the three-year rule. One gradually builds up a large number of capable men and women who have served in this highest of offices, who know the detailed workings of the parish from inside knowledge and whose experience is of immense value both to the incumbent and the parish as a whole. In one parish, when I had eight or nine such people, I formed them into a body of elders. I described this purely unofficial scheme in my book *The Parish Seeks The Way* (Mowbray, 1960, page 85). Of course women can and should be elected to this office.

It is also an excellent rule for each PCC member to stand down after completing three years of service. They should be asked to stand down for one year. By this means new blood is constantly introduced. In a flourishing parish there is rarely any difficulty about getting the three-year rule (which must be entirely voluntary and unofficial) accepted by virtually everybody but in parishes with small populations (or small congregations) there are obvious difficulties.

How do you step up attendance at the annual meeting? A personal invitation signed by the vicar can be sent to everybody whose name is on the roll. This will certainly produce gratifying results, for it makes clear to all that they are wanted. Some churches have the meeting on a Sunday morning immediately after service and this brings excellent results in parishes where congregations are large and attendance at the annual meeting tends otherwise to be very small. Perhaps the best way of all is to ensure that the meeting itself is lively, well organized and neither dull nor over long. The vicar should spend little time in looking back and more time in looking forward, saying something about the sort of things he wants the new PCC to consider and perhaps one or two of his own cherished convictions relating to the year ahead.

It really is helpful if speakers from the floor take part in discussions and they should be encouraged to do so. In some parishes a pleasant custom obtains of a senior member (often a church officer) thanking the incumbent and his wife for all they have done during the year. The incumbent will already have warmly thanked the curate, the non-stipendiary priest, the reader (and their wives) and of course the leading officers. A word of thanks now and again is much appreciated.

(6) *The Parochial Church Council*

The incumbent is required to call at least four meetings of the PCC a year—and if there are only four they should be quarterly. Probably a monthly meeting in busier parishes will be found necessary. Its duties are defined by the Synodical Government Measure 1969 as: 'It shall be the duty of the incumbent and the Parochial Church Council to consult together on matters of general concern and importance to the parish'. The functions include 'co-operation with the incumbent in promoting in the parish the whole mission of the Church, pastoral, evangelistic, social and ecumenical'. For full details of the Measure (legal requirements, powers, procedures and much else) the reader should refer to *A Handbook for Churchwardens and Parochial Church Councillors* (Mowbray, 1983).

The incumbent is ex-officio chairman; some incumbents say that they dread the meetings of the PCC. Sometimes it is the triviality of the proceedings that fills them with dismay, sometimes the obsession with money matters, sometimes rather angry scenes as members differ emphatically from each other. A good chairman can avoid at least some of these pitfalls. First of all he should know how to conduct a meeting. There are perfectly definite rules about procedure and these are clearly set out in *A Handbook for Churchwardens and Parochial Church Councillors*. Then he should know what is on the agenda and what issues are likely to be raised. He ought not to be weak, like putty in the hands of his higher powered members, but equally he should avoid being a dictator determined to have his own way. He must on no account talk too much himself but rather should give the impression that he very much wants to hear what all have to say. Naturally there will be issues on which he holds views, perhaps strong views, but it is not always wise to announce them at the beginning. It is far better to give everybody a chance to make out a case for perhaps precisely the opposite of what the incumbent really wants. Decisions must be made by the meeting and not by the chairman; but the chairman can sum up at the end of a debate and declare what he believes the right decision to be. In some matters he would do better to leave the decision entirely to the good sense of the meeting, for if the meeting senses that he trusts them this can be immensely helpful.

(7) *The Umbrella Committee System*

All the emphasis now is on synodical government, a process that involves the laity in decision making to a far greater extent than used to be the case. How can we best make use of the talents of PCC members? One way is to divide the PCC into 'umbrella' committees, each with its own lay chairman and secretary; all these committee would meet on the same evening in the same hall, alternating with meetings of the full council.

I described this umbrella committee system in two articles in the *Church Times* (5 November 1965 and 17 March 1972) and of all the many articles of mine printed in that valuable paper these occasioned far more letters than any others. The system has been widely adopted by many parishes, with of course local variations.

In Guildford we had three of these PCC committees—church buildings, internal affairs and external affairs. All PCC members at the first meeting after the annual general meeting were asked to state their first and second preferences and it was always an easy matter to form the committees. The clergy and churchwardens were ex-officio members of all three so that they could be present whenever any item required their presence.

We decided that the full PCC and the umbrella committees would meet on alternate months. The chairmen of the umbrella committees are the key figures. I wanted them to be elected but it was decided that they should always be chosen by the incumbent. Vice-chairmen and secretaries were elected by each committee. At first the committees presented their recommendations to the next full meeting of the PCC. It was found better for each committee evening to end with a meeting of the full PCC lasting about half-an-hour. The recommendations were nearly always (but not invariably) approved.

We of course had a finance and standing committee that also met once a month. The chairmen joined the other church officers to form it. The agenda for the umbrella committees was always drawn up by this body. What did each committee do? We had many church buildings, some in rather a poor state. The church buildings committee made one member responsible for each one, with the full approval of the churchwardens. After a few years every single one of our church buildings had received attention and eventually all were in sound condition. Internal affairs covered all that went on in the parish—the services, the music, the monthly magazine, the weekly newsletter, parish organizations, social occasions, outings, parties, work with children and young people and so on. I remember occasions when leaders of particular organizations were invited to appear before the committee to say what was being done, what the objects were and in what ways the PCC could help. External affairs covered the areas of concern that it was felt ought to be kept in the forefront—the work of the Church overseas, outward giving (this committee always made detailed recommendations of what should be given to whom), the ecumenical scene, the local Council of Churches, Christian Aid, the third world, town events, diocesan affairs and much else. Members of this committee represented us on the various Councils and brought back informative reports.

It should not be supposed that the incumbent loses anything important by this method of ordering parochial affairs. It is true he has to surrender some of his ancient prerogatives. If the incumbent holds that it is his right alone to determine what services should be held and when, whether any music should be allowed, what societies should be supported and precisely how all buildings should be heated, lit and cleaned, then he had better not make use of it. But if he holds strongly that laymen should be given very real authority to make decisions and carry them out, if he is willing to sit under a lay chairman, if he wants to harness the talent to be found in almost every congregation, if he wishes to come right into line with synodical principles, then there may well be something here for him. Neither he nor the parish loses anything. Both gain much.

(8) *Waywardens*

It is a useful extension of the principle of parish partnership to involve the laity as waywardens. At its simplest, the aim of the waywarden system is to have one church representative in every street in the parish. This representative reports to the vicar every Sunday after morning service with information about any event that has occurred in the street on a form like this:

WAYWARDEN'S RETURN FOR WEEK ENDING ....
     Street ....
     Any sick or deaths ....
     Any newcomers...
     Any special visits needed ....

I have been looking at a full description of the Waywardens scheme that I described fully in my *The Parish Seeks the Way* (Mowbray, 1960) and I see I said: 'The whole scheme began splendidly, but the usual difficulties were experienced as the years went on. Some faithful ones never failed us, but the enthusiasm of some others began to dwindle and they became slack and careless'. This is an occupational hazard in the life of any parish priest and at times firm action has to be taken. In this case we packed up the whole scheme and began again from scratch, re-using the effective members and quietly dropping the ineffective ones. It *can* be done without upsetting anybody—and certainly without attracting unhelpful headlines in the local newspaper!

It is highly desirable that the waywardens should also be the parish magazine distributors and thus call every month on many of the houses. They can display an attractively designed card in the window. They can distribute letters from the vicar, some to church members only, some to every house. They can have a small notice board for putting up the weekly church poster. They can encourage (and call for) people to come along to services, young people to join the youth club, even confirmation candidates to come to classes. As it grows there is much to be said for area secretaries for, say, every eight streets and one general secretary in charge of all waywardens. If people see the point of all this fairly elaborate organization they will agree to serve when approached by the vicar himself. Many of them will carry out the duties with wonderful efficiency; but there will be a few who will not and these must be tactfully replaced. It is not enough just to find the right people; they must be trained for this important service.

(9) *Finding Leaders*

Much of the work of the incumbent consists of finding and training people for jobs. He is not only looking for people he can put into key positions in the parish organizations. He should also keep an eye out for readers, men or women who have a genuine vocation to serve and who when trained and licensed can be invaluable adjuncts in almost every type of parish. Readers take an enormous number of services throughout the country every Sunday and their faithfulness and devotion are beyond all praise. The parish priest is also on the look out for ordinands. Often it is he who puts the idea into the head of a suitable candidate. Who knows better than the parish priest which of the young men in the parish might have precisely the right qualities to answer God's call?

There may well be men (and, hopefully, women) who are devout members and who feel that God is calling them to the part-time non-stipendiary ministry. The ordination to the priesthood of many such people has already made an immense difference to the running of parishes where the incumbent would otherwise be run off his feet.

Chapter 4

The Parson's Pay and Conditions of Service

(1) *How the Clergy are Paid*

You rarely hear the clergy complaining in public about being underpaid. They knew, when they offered for ordination, that it would mean accepting a lower standard than people receive in other professions or occupations. They see the job as a vocation, not as a career. Nevertheless the clergy have to pay their bills like everybody else and they want to maintain their wives and children in reasonable comfort. Inflation affects those on fixed incomes more than those who are not and it is probably true that parsons are feeling the pinch at the present time to a greater extent than many of their fellows.

A diocesan bishop told me recently that he reckoned all his clergy ought to be able to manage on the present stipend scheme approved by the General Synod and nearly all were doing so. True, some wives have full or part-time jobs, but I suspect the majority of clergy wives do not. How I would have hated it if mine had—and how much my various parishes would have suffered! The chief reason why things are far easier than they used to be is that it is standard practice for a PCC to meet the reasonable and necessary expenses of office of their clergy. Not so many years ago this was the exception rather than the rule. In many a parish the clergy (incumbent and assistant clergy) fill in a monthly form claiming expenses.

The other great bugbear used to be compulsory residence in what might be a huge Victorian semi-mansion. The incumbent was responsible for the costs of heating and lighting and general upkeep, including interior decoration and garden maintenance. The alternatives were dreary shabbiness or constant financial strain. Now every diocese is selling these huge, unsuitable parsonages (often for a very handsome figure) and replacing them with much smaller but perfectly adequate ones. Curiously, this is often not possible until a vacancy occurs. The resident incumbent has got used to his large house and vast garden and neither he nor his parishioners want to part with it. They like having committee meetings in the house and fetes in the garden. But the full cost of quinquennial repairs falls upon the diocesan Board of Finance and it is obviously most unfair for this often very substantial charge to be paid; pressure to sell unsuitable parsonage houses is unlikely to ease up.

How is the incumbent paid? What are his sources of income? They used to be many and varied. There were parish endowments (in some parishes very large, in others almost negligible). There was glebe income (again, in some rural parishes this was substantial but in most nothing at all). There were fees for weddings and funerals, etc., and an Easter offering. All this has now changed. Fees are received but not kept. The Easter offering is for the clergy as a whole and not for the incumbent. This being so, many parishes have dropped it. This is a pity. It is good for there to be an annual opportunity for faithful worshippers to show their appreciation of the clergy of the diocese and not for their own man. I know of one diocese, when this scheme was introduced, where the income from Easter offerings went up substantially, to the benefit of all.

Now practically all incumbents in a diocese receive precisely the same, although dioceses do differ from each other. This may now have been put right; at any rate the 1983 McLean Report said: 'differing stipend levels between dioceses as a matter of principle are difficult to defend on any rational basis'. In a diocese all incumbents receive the same because there is no such thing as an 'important' parish. All of them are important because in all of them God's work is being done. Thus the Vicar of, say, Leeds (with vast responsibilities) must be paid precisely the same as the Rector of Little Snoring in the Wold. The official view is that there is no career structure in our Church.

It is difficult to find fault with this argument, although there is no way of ensuring that all incumbents receive the same. As I said, some clergy wives work full-time, earning perhaps far more than their husbands, but there is no way of taking this into account. Some are able to take in summer visitors on a bed-and-breakfast basis if their parishes are in attractive holiday areas. In London (for instance) rooms in the parsonage can be let at hefty rents. Incumbents can write books and articles and receive money for doing it. There is no way of taking these things into account. It remains a fact of life that some are more equal than others.

Actually there *is* a career structure. It begins to operate when a man becomes a residentiary canon, when his stipend increases slightly. It increases quite a lot when he becomes an archdeacon, even more when he becomes a dean. A suffragan bishop goes sharply up, a diocesan bishop even more so (quite dramatically if he happens to be Bishop of London, Durham or Winchester). These increases are presumably not a reflection of increased responsibility. The assumption is that dignitaries must enjoy a higher standard of living and thus stipend differentials are reflected in retirement pensions.

There is really no way of altering this. General Synod decides such matters of policy and the Central Stipends

Authority carry out the wishes expressed. General Synod is clear that present practice is the best way and most clergy accept this. I can think of one exception. It was a deacon who came to me for training and at a diocesan conference he caused a stir by declaring in ringing tones: 'There is no career structure in the Church, nor should there be. There should be no differentials in terms of salary. We ought all to be paid a reasonable living wage, no more, whether we are junior deacons or archbishops. The differentials should come in the payment of expenses'. This remarkable statement made the headlines in the local newspaper. We were all very amused by this youthful indiscretion—but on what grounds would anybody say he was wrong?

(2) *Central Stipends Authority*

Incumbents used to be paid by tithes paid by farmers and land owners. These have been phased out. A tithe rent charge was substituted in 1936 and after that year it was collected by the State on behalf of the clergy. In many parishes what was called the greater tithe was paid to the rector, who might appoint somebody *in vicarius* to do the actual work. He received the lesser tithe for doing it. The old distinction between rector and vicar has now gone but the titles remain. Now the Central Stipends Authority takes care of all stipend matters.

The General Synod in 1972 decided to set up a Central Stipends Authority (CSA) and asked the Church Commissioners to undertake this duty. The full details of the scheme can be found in *Central Stipends Authority Regulations* 1982 (GS 109) but the main items can be summarized briefly.

The CSA shall keep under review and adjust as appropriate the stipends of diocesan bishops, deans, provosts and residentiary canons and the augmentation of suffragan and assistant bishops and archdeacons. It will consult diocesan authorities and advise them on the forms and levels of the pay of clergymen, deaconesses and licensed lay workers. It will submit for the approval of the General Synod such payment schemes as it may consider appropriate. It will determine the distribution among dioceses of funds available to it for stipends and lay down conditions on which such funds shall be paid into diocesan stipends funds. The CSA will have power to obtain from diocesan authorities whatever information it may require concerning their stipends arrangements and resources. It will give directions to diocesan authorities when necessary on the forms and levels of pay, and perhaps most important of all, it will lay down standard terms and common methods to be used by diocesan authorities in computing incomes.

The McClean Report (GS 498, 1981) suggests various changes, one of which is that the CSA should listen to the views of the dioceses and not just say what is to be done. This report was duly received by General Synod, when great gratitude to the CSA was recorded. No very major changes were recommended.

All glebe rents have been pooled, and objections raised in General Synod that this does not honour the wishes of the original benefactors were not upheld. The anomalies were becoming a scandal.

A brief word about the resources of the Church Commissioners may be of interest. They controlled assets worth in 1982 about £1,228m (they were worth less than half this in 1976) and these produced an income of about £90m in that year (more than double the 1976 income). In other words our capital assets are superbly managed. Some further interesting facts emerge from the McClean Report. In 1980 the payroll of the clergy numbered about 11,500 and of the stipends the Church Commissioners contributed 53 per cent and the dioceses and parishes 34 per cent, the remaining 13 per cent coming from fees, etc. Sometimes you hear it said that by the nineties *all* the resources of the Church Commissioners will be needed to pay clergy pensions, leaving the whole cost of clergy remuneration to be borne by parishioners. The Church Commissioners do not take this view. It seems that the official view is that the number of pensioners will stabilize within the next few years and then remain steady for the rest of the century. But it is certainly true that a higher proportion of clergy pay will have to be found by parishioners.

Those who want more detailed information can obtain it from the annual *Church Commissioners Report and Accounts*, copies of which are circulated to interested parties. There is also *Central Stipends Authority. Tenth Report* (GS Misc. 160) which appeared in 1982 and which contains charts and diagrams that bring life to rather dull figures and make a lot of facts absorbingly interesting.

(3) *Parsonage House and Other Benefits*

In addition to stipend there are benefits in kind which the incumbent enjoys. The chief of these is a free parsonage house, with repairs, rates, exterior decoration and insurance all entirely free. Some clergy regard this as a doubtful asset because it means that they do not live in a house of their own and thus lose the great benefit of capital appreciation that so many house owners in their parishes are fortunate enough to receive. Moreover, they may have no house to which their widows may go in the event of their untimely death or no house to which to retire when the time comes. This last point is now being well taken care of, as we will see in a later section. The fact remains that an incumbent can reckon on living in a far better house than he would be likely to buy for himself and he is protected against the ever-increasing maintenance costs that most people have to bear. In 1983 it was reckoned that the free house together with tax advantages for heating and lighting and garden upkeep (which most people do not receive) together with a non-contributory pension were worth at least £3,000 a year.

(4) *Expenses of Office*

One great change can now be taken for granted. When I was first ordained it was unusual for any parish to pay any considerable proportion of the incumbent's expenses of office, indeed most parishes paid nothing at all. Now it is common for the parish to pay 90 per cent or more and this makes all the difference between managing and not managing. Expenses of curates, deaconesses and stipendiary lay workers are also payable in full.

The properly reimbursable parochial expenses of the clergy include postages, stationery, telephone, car (running and depreciation), provision and depreciation of office equipment, maintenance of robes, hospitality and provision for a locum tenens. The official list also includes the cost of secretarial assistance but this is about as sensible as counting the salary of the organist and verger. The secretary is employed by and for the parish and should be paid direct, not by the incumbent but by the PCC.

Costs of heating, lighting, cleaning and garden upkeep, not to mention the salary which any incumbent can pay to his wife for receptionist and other duties, are not treated as PCC expenses but can be claimed as expenses qualifying for income tax relief. The wife of course has actually to be paid. It is not a notional payment.

I say it is common for clergy expenses to be reimbursed practically in full. There are cases where this is far from being the case, partly because of the incumbent's unwillingness to claim, partly because of an unsympathetic PCC and partly because of sheer lack of funds. It is doubtful whether any diocesan bishop would be willing to institute a man to any living where the expenses of office were not paid. By the way, a well-to-do incumbent who refuses to accept anything at all in expenses is not to be congratulated on his astonishing generosity but rather rebuked for making things impossible for his successor.

How should expenses be precisely quantified and claimed?

A post book should be kept and receipts always obtained when stationery (or anything else likely to be claimed) is purchased. The PCC should pay the telephone bill, with the incumbent paying an estimated sum for his own (and his family's) calls. Receipts for renewed robes should of course be produced. Perhaps hospitality expenses are the most difficult to calculate and probably it is best for the PCC to make a modest entertainment allowance available. PCC's should ensure that the expenses of visiting clergy are always offered and the appropriate fees paid when visiting clergy are required to help out in times of sickness or holiday.

It is car expenses that are easily the heaviest item. Expenses should include not only the bare cost of petrol used on parish business but also a proportion of the licence, insurance, repairs and depreciation costs. The clergyman must keep a log of journeys made and every PCC should be urged to accept the composite mileage allowance recommended by the Central Stipends Authority each year and approved by the diocese and Inland Revenue. A man who runs a tiny car will score, while the man who insists on something large, fast and powerful will lose. Some parishes may think it unreasonable to be charged for mileage used on diocesan as opposed to parish business but a generous view is usually taken by the PCC if they know that the alternative is for their incumbent to have to pay himself. All payment of expenses has obviously got to be with the approval of the Income Tax inspector. My experience has been that all such people are most helpful and understanding provided that documentary evidence can be produced to support statements made.

There is an excellent booklet called *The Parochial Expenses of the Clergy* published by the CSA in 1982 and it ought to be carefully studied by all clergy, deaconesses, licensed lay workers, churchwardens and parish treasurers. On the back page there is a sample monthly claims form that is simplicity itself. It is reproduced here by permission. There is no other really satisfactory way of ensuring the fair and reasonable repayment of parish expenses.

SAMPLE MONTHLY CLAIMS FORM

PARISH OF...
(NB: For multi parish cures, this form will probably require minor amendment)

CLAIM FOR REIMBURSEMENT OF EXPENSES INCURRED BY........................
.... IN MONTH OF.. 19.......

PLEASE READ THE NOTES BELOW BEFORE COMPLETING THE FORM

USE OF CAR .... MILES *(a* .... p PER MILE   See Note 3
PUBLIC TRANSPORT
TELEPHONE — rental (in full)
          — calls (less £   for private use)
POSTAGE AND STATIONERY
OFFICE EQUIPMENT
          (DETAILED BELOW)
ROBES
BOOKS
HOSPITALITY
TRAINING — Course fees and expenses
FEES AND EXPENSES PAID TO LOCUM TENENS
   AND OTHER   See Note 4
SECRETARIAL ASSISTANCE
MISCELLANEOUS (SPECIFIED)   ....
                               ....
                               ....
                               ....
                               TOTAL EXPENDITURE

SIGNED...(CLERGYMAN) ....(DATE)
SIGNED...(PCC TREASURER)............................(DATE)

NOTES:
(1) All expenses necessarily incurred in connection with parochial, deanery and diocesan duties should be claimed. Any expenses incurred in connection with other duties, such as chaplaincies, may also be included if no provision is made for them by any other authority. The cost of heating, lighting and cleaning the parsonage and of garden upkeep should not be included. **In any case of doubt the diocesan office should be consulted.**
(2) The clergyman, etc., and the parochial church council concerned should discuss regularly the likely level of claims under any of the headings shown.
(3) The mileage rate should be that recommended by the diocese on the advice of the CSA and the Inland Revenue.
(4) These should be at the rate recommended by the diocese.
(5) A copy of this form should be retained by the clergyman for use in connnection with his Annual Return to the diocese and any claim he may make to the Inland Revenue for tax relief on any proportion of expenses not reimbursed.

If clergy expenses are met in full by the PCC then filling in the annual Income Tax return ought to be a fairly simple matter. Some find this task daunting. It is usually possible to find a qualified accountant locally who does this sort of thing for a modest charge. I have always found it money well spent to employ such a person. He sees to it that all that can be properly claimed is claimed. If any queries crop up he can deal with them. That useful periodical *Which?* has ample evidence that people commonly pay too much in income tax. There is a leaflet called *Taxation of Ministers of Religion* that can be obtained from the Church Commissioners. It ought to be known that all clergy tax affairs are dealt with by HM Inspector of Taxes, East 1 District, Parsons Estate, Washington, Tyne and Wear NE37 1HE.

(5) *National Insurance*

For National Insurance purposes clergymen, deaconesses and licensed lay workers are classified as 'employed earners'. As such we are liable for Class 1 National Insurance contributions and we are not in the state Earnings Related Pensions scheme. It is not precisely defined who are our employers but the Church Commissioners have been designated as the 'secondary contributor'.

Class 1 contributions are deducted monthly by the Commissioners from the monthly stipend cheque and they are based upon our taxable pay or 'reckonable earnings' received from the CSA. If local income is also received (say as a hospital chaplain) the position is slightly complicated and reference should be made to the secretary of the board of finance. The fees you receive, for example, may be made reckonable for National Insurance purposes. National Insurance contributions, like PAYE, are based upon reckonable earnings paid by the CSA and a Class 1 contributor becomes eligible for the various state benefits after a time.

Sickness benefit is one of these. If you are ill and cannot carry out your duties, the Commissioners pay the first eight weeks of sickness benefit in any one year or in any period of continuous sickness. This system is known as 'statutory' sick pay and is subject to both PAYE and National Insurance contributions. You can claim if you are ill for at least four consecutive days. During the eight weeks you receive exactly the same amount as usual but *not* the statutory sick pay in addition. The idea is that we ought not to be better off ill than when we are at work. The CSA recovers all money due in respect of our sickness claims. It is used to help our diocesan stipends fund.

(6) *Clergy Pensions and Housing*

The Church of England Pensions Board was constituted as the pensions authority for the Church of England as long ago as 1926 and is responsible for the pensions of clergy who have served in the provinces of Canterbury and York and for their widows and dependants, also for deaconesses and licensed lay workers. A full pension is paid for thirty-seven or more years of pensionable service and a proportionate pension for more than five years of pensionable service. A disability pension can be granted on retirement before the age of sixty-five if the Pensions Board is satisfied that such retirement is necessary because of permanent ill-health.

If a pensioner has a gross income from all sources (including that of his wife but disregarding the State pension and £300 worth of earnings) of less than the maximum basic pension, he qualifies for a supplementary pension. All clergymen receive a tax-free payment on retirement in addition to their pension. If a clergyman dies after the age of sixty-five but before retirement, the lump sum is payable to his estate. If he dies before sixty-five there will be a payment to his widow from the Central Church Group Term Insurance Scheme (and this payment is much greater than the retirement grant) if his diocese was sensible enough to join this scheme, which is controlled by the Ecclesiastical Insurance Office.

The Pensions Board publish a most helpful booklet called *Your Pension Rights*, which answers all the questions commonly asked. All clergy should also study *The Clergy Voluntary Contributions Scheme*, a booklet containing details of voluntary pension contributions that became effective on 1 January 1983. Once you start paying your monthly contribution you will be expected to carry on paying up to age sixty-five. There are tax advantages. A man who pays £10 a month for twenty-five years can expect to receive on retirement £20,256. This is one of many examples quoted in the booklet.

It is also very gratifying to know that the retirement housing of the clergy (or their widows) has now been taken in hand in such a way that no worries remain. It used to be a considerable worry. I am one of those who voted in General Synod for the compulsory retirement of all clergy at the age of seventy (we were told, however, that in the view of the Crown lawyers this could only apply to those appointed to a job after January 1976 since you cannot take away a life freehold once given). Unfortunately we did not then consider just where the retired clergyman was going to live. We hoped existing arrangements would prove to be adequate. It soon became clear that they were not.

In 1983 a new scheme came into operation which surely meets every need. It gives to all full-time clergy, deaconesses and licensed lay workers who can expect to receive a pension an assurance that there will be available financial assistance for retirement housing. All those eligible may apply for a mortgage up to three years before normal retirement age. There are now several options open. The Pensions Board own over 800 properties and one might be available in the desired area at an agreed rent. Sometimes the Board will purchase a property of your choice and charge an agreed rent. But it is the mortgage scheme (called Equity Sharing) that will appear to most. If you are a tenant then rules may apply that you find undesirable whereas if you purchase on mortgage you make the rules. Those who purchase a house on mortgage of course have to meet rate charges, water rates, insurance and all maintenance, repair and decoration charges. But as the mortgage cost is very low indeed it is obviously well worth going into. A booklet called *Finance for Retirement Housing* (obtainable from the Pensions Board) gives all the details. The mortgage costs 3 per cent in the first year.

All this adds up to a retirement free from housing or financial worries. True, there are other worries. Some clergy complain of feeling unwanted and not being made welcome at chapter meetings. Retired clergy should certainly join the Retired clergy Association (the address of the honorary secretary is London Diocesan House, 30 Causton Street, London SW1P 4AU) and attend the branch meetings if there are any. Efforts are being made to establish branches in every diocese.

Those who retire when fit and full of energy may consider taking on a part-time curacy. The *Church Times* often contains an advertisement offering a suitable house rent free in exchange for Sunday duty plus perhaps some pastoral work. Frequently expenses are offered as well. The snag is that you may become unfit—and what then? Or you may die—then what does your widow do? Snags there are but I have known several who have made this arrangement, to the mutual advantage of both the incumbent and the retired man.

(7) *Conditions of Service*

Much helpful information about the parish priest's legal position and his conditions of service will be found in *A Handbook for Churchwardens and Parochial Church Councillors* (Mowbray, 1983). Nowadays it is common for a man to be appointed priest-in-charge of a benefice when the future of the benefice is being considered but the normal procedure is (or ought to be) institution by the bishop and induction by the archdeacon (or deputy appointed by the bishop). Institution admits to the cure of souls and induction to the property rights.

Certain duties have to be performed. He must say Morning and Evening Prayer daily and celebrate Holy Communion on all Sundays and greater feast days and Ash Wednesday. He must administer the sacrament and other rites (including baptisms, marriages and burials). If for any reason he refuses to baptize a baby who is a parishioner the parents can appeal to the bishop, who will give such directions as he thinks fit (Canon B.22.2). He must preach a sermon or cause one to be preached at least once a Sunday. He must prepare and present candidates for confirmation, be diligent in visiting his parishioners and provide opportunities for them to resort to him for spiritual counsel and advice. He can arrange for others to carry out these duties and he may be excused from some of them by his bishop. Full details will be found in Canons B11 and C24, indeed a careful reading of all the Canons of the Church of England is strongly recommended. Editions appeared in 1969, 1975 and 1981. We are even told what we should wear at Morning and Evening Prayer, at the Occasional Offices and at Holy Communion (Canon B8). How many of us know that Canon F5 requires that 'in every church and chapel surplices shall be provided and maintained in a clean condition for the use of the minister'?

Now that we have *The Alternative Services Book 1980* there are certain decisions that must be made and certain courses of action that must be adopted. More will be said about this later. It should be noted that by the terms of the Prayer Book (Alternative and Other Services) Measure 1965 the minister is empowered to make variations 'not of substantial importance' in authorized forms of service. This Measure has now been repealed but Canon B5.1 still stands.

The incumbent must reside in his parish unless he has the bishop's licence not to do so and if he fails to reside for the required period in any year (nine months) he may have to forfeit part of his stipend. If he is absent for a whole year without permission the benefice becomes vacant. It should be added that it seems to be beoming increasingly general for a parson to have a 'sabbatical' every now and again, when of course the above rules would not operate. The incumbent ceases to have any right to the emoluments of the parish on the date his incumbency ceases. When he dies the widow must vacate the parsonage house within two calendar months but it should not be supposed that widows are severely treated at such times. Every possible form of help is available and every effort made to ease the burden.

An assistant curate has security of office once licensed by the bishop and he cannot be dismissed except with the bishop's consent. The assistant curate may resign on giving three months' notice to the incumbent. A new incumbent may dismiss an assistant curate within six months of his induction provided he gives six weeks' notice.

A clergyman may be tried in the ecclesiastical courts and dispossessed of his benefice for (1) conduct unbecoming the office and work of a clerk in holy orders and (2) serious, persistent or continuous neglect of duty. The procedure is so cumbersome and so expensive that it is very unlikely to be invoked except in the most blatant cases; such cases are, mercifully, exceedingly rare.

Chapter 5

Parish Income

(1) *The Parish Treasurer*

Normally the PCC appoints a treasurer at the first meeting after the annual meeting. He is usually somebody who is an expert at book-keeping or who has some professional interest in money matters.

The treasurer receives, banks and accounts for all parish income and settles all authorized accounts. It is the duty of the PCC to 'furnish to the annual meeting an account made up to 31 December immediately preceding such meeting, setting out the council's income and expenditure during the year, together with a statement of the funds and property, if any, remaining in its hands at the date of the account. This account and statement having been duly audited must be submitted for approval at such meeting . . .' (Halsbury's Laws 3rd Edition Vol 13 Para. 352). It is a relief to many incumbents that they are not responsible for doing this but a wise man will make himself familiar with the whole basis of Christian giving in his parish and with the main items of income and expenditure. Both giving and expenditure provide useful temperature charts from which the spiritual health of the parish may be gauged.

The whole concept of Christian giving has changed and there can be few incumbents who can 'leave all that sort of thing to the laity' while they get on with what they reckon to be their real job. The plain fact is that diocesan quotas are so enormous that in some parishes there is all too little left for other things. The great bulk of the quota is needed for the payment of the clergy. It should be known that in 1983, for the first time, the contribution of the Church Commissioners towards the cost of clergy stipends fell below 50 per cent. They contributed 49 per cent whereas contributions from local sources (including the parishes and glebe) amounted to 51 per cent. This percentage is bound to rise, not fall, because an increasing proportion of the Church Commissioners' income will be required for clergy pensions.

(2) *Traditional Methods of Fund Raising*

In Victorian days the squire and the gentry were usually the prime (and in some cases the only) source of money, which is why so many old parish magazines featured the names of benefactors with obsequious expressions of thanks. There was no question among the givers of not letting your left hand know what your right hand was doing. The wealthy gave, often very generously, but they liked everyone to know about it.

When giving spread from the few to the many, things like the annual summer fête and the Christmas bazaar became two of the most important events of the year, for upon their success depended the whole running of the parish. People liked to give, but not always directly. Often more was required, and moving appeals for more in the collection bag tended to fall upon deaf ears. Accordingly the clergy themselves had to think out and work for all sorts of money-raising schemes. There were seemingly endless jumble sales, whist drives, miles of pennies and so on. Often the vicar sat in the church porch all day, begging bowl in hand. It was not always very dignified or very successful. But a movement that originated in America reached this country in the fifties and soon began to change the whole face of money raising for church expenses.

(3) *Christian Stewardship*

The movement was termed planned giving. It was pioneered by Colonel Wells and promoted by the Wells Organization. It just so happened that my Bristol parish had the first Wells campaign in that diocese and I thus saw at close range the whole thing in action in its very early days. This is the sort of thing that happened in my parish and in very many others as long ago as 1958.

A highly trained and highly paid professional fund-raiser came to live in the parish for perhaps a month or so. The basic fee for his services might have been as high as £200 a week. He insisted on being provided with a parish office, a full time competent shorthand typist, a telephone, a typewriter, a duplicator and an adding machine. It was one of his jobs to train a body of men to visit everybody in the area likely to contribute to church funds. Impressive invitations to a splendid free dinner were taken by hand to all whose names were listed. The campaign was launched at the dinner by four speakers and a glossy brochure was distributed. Then the visitors paid personal calls to persuade people to pledge the maximum possible amount. The standard set was the biblical tithe and people were asked to get as close to it as they could. The incumbent was responsible for drawing up the list of people to approach and he had to announce in church his own personal pledge which had to be large, to encourage the others.

Results could be sensational. Often the giving of the parish doubled or more. In 1956 the ordinary income of all parishes totalled £13,422,000. In 1962 it totalled £22,393,000. In 1966 the figure was over £27m and this had risen in 1970 to no less than £37,563,604.

These figures may seem very unimpressive now but all those years ago it was obvious that something very remarkable was happening, something that in parish after parish was altering all previously held ideas about financing church work.

Few can doubt that the credit for the increased giving must go to the planned giving movement; curiously, there were always objectors both among the clergy and the laity. It was felt that it was all too American, not in very good taste, not the sort of way we did things in this country, too reminiscent of big-business methods and not consistent with the doing of God's work. There was certainly an element of what Colonel Wells termed 'pocket-book protection'. A lot of well-to-do people strongly objected to others knowing what they gave. This was not engaging modesty because they gave so much. It was much more likely to be shame at the sheer triviality of their weekly gift.

There were further objections. A great feature of the original planned giving campaigns was an undertaking to do away with the fêtes, the bazaars, the jumble sales and so on because they would no longer be necessary. But people missed these things. Pensioners and others of limited means could give generously of their time and talents in making things for stalls, and many a parish reckoned it was the poorer for cutting out eagerly-awaited social occasions. There was also a feeling that the Church of England was becoming far too money conscious and in danger of giving the impression that this was the one matter with which we were most deeply concerned.

Thus in the early seventies it became apparent that dioceses were tending to discourage the professional fund-raising organizations. At first they appointed their own professional lay directors, available to any parish that needed their expertise. After some years they tended to get rid of them and appoint instead part-time clergymen who were also given small parishes to provide them with a house and stipend. In some cases unpaid laymen were appointed who certainly had the necessary Christian convictions and the enthusiasm, but not the skills. The result was fewer and fewer campaigns and those that were held were often not very successful.

In the eighties it became apparent that things were on the

move again. More and more dioceses were advertising in the *Church Times* for full-time trained lay persons to act as stewardship directors. The term 'planned giving' was gradually dropped and 'Christian stewardship' took its place. Obviously it must be right for stewardship of time and talents to be exercised but when full-scale stewardship campaigns are held, often after much careful preparation and considerable expense, many of us have learned in the hard school of experience that it is best to concentrate on money only. Otherwise it seems to be omitted. A good way is to have another campaign to deal with time and talents.

It is also noticeable that fêtes and bazaars are right back in the picture but a lot of parishes give away the total proceeds. Sponsored efforts of all kinds are common—sponsored runs, sponsored swims, sponsored sing-ins, sponsored almost anything. Each year it becomes more and more necessary for our Church to increase its giving and it stands out a mile that this will continue. The prospects are daunting, what with the diocesan quota, the payment of clerical expenses, and perhaps the roof leaking, the organ on its last legs and the heating system worn out. But a former Archbishop of Canterbury (Dr Coggan) surely had it right when he said something to the effect that we are a Church, not a business concern. Somehow when our priorities are right, when projects are prayed about, when all is done in the name of God, financial difficulties have a strange habit of solving themselves. This was his experience over many years.

The Central Board of Finance has a Christian Stewardship Committee through which it promotes co-ordination, mutual support and interchange of ideas among the Christian Stewardship organizations of the dioceses. It is responsible for conferences, publications and personal liaison. One publication is a leaflet called *A Responding Church* (obtainable from the Church House Bookshop, Great Smith Street, London SW1P 3BN) and it certainly ought to be in every church. It sets out the principles of Christian stewardship very clearly, including the fact that the minimum standard of giving commended by Bishops and the General Synod is 5 per cent or £1 of every £20 of weekly income. It also says that tithing, the giving of £1 of every £10 is 'a time-honoured and more exacting standard for total giving'.

Some useful books about money-raising include *A Theology of Generosity* by W. W. Badger Berrie (Mowbray, 1981) and *Tithing* by R. T. Kendall (Hodder and Stoughton, 1982).

(4) *The Annual Budget*

Whether the incumbent likes it or not, he is bound to be concerned with parish income. True, all the collecting and accounting are done by laymen who know about these things. But he has to teach his people that there is a spiritual side that must not be ignored. If he gives the impression that he cares but little he is going to have problems.

A budget is necessary. One should be drawn up by the Finance Committee and approved by the PCC and presented to the annual meeting. The Parochial Church Councils (Powers) Measure 1956 states: 'The Council of every parish shall have power to frame an annual budget of moneys required for the maintenance of the work of the Church in the parish and otherwise and to take such steps as they think necessary for the raising, collecting and allocating of such moneys'.

Of course this involves sorting out priorities. The first priority must of course be the diocesan quota, to be paid promptly when due (usually quarterly) and always in full. Treasurers should be discouraged from hanging on to the money until the last possible moment because that way they get the benefit of interest. This is surely unethical, to say the least, and only makes the work of the diocesan office more difficult. The next priority might well be the payment of clergy expenses of office, for unless this is done it is an item that tends to drop lower and lower in the scale of essentials.

Most of the clergy will not press for this item to be high on the list. Others should do the pressing for them. Domestic affairs come next—heating the church, for instance, and seeing that buildings are in good repair and that everything used in worship is in excellent condition.

After this attention must be paid to giving away. We must avoid at all costs selfishness and concentration on our own local set-up. It was another Archbishop of Canterbury (Dr William Temple) who said that the Church that lives for itself will die by itself.

It is not difficult for a stewardship parish to frame a budget. It knows roughly what its income is likely to be. This will be the total amount pledged by members of the planned giving scheme, the income tax refund obtained from covenants, the estimated loose collections and money raised by special efforts. The great bulk of this will be from the first two items. With this information before them the Finance Committee should be able to draw up a budget of necessary expenditure, present it to the PCC for full and free discussion and produce something clear and straightforward for the annual meeting. It might look something like this:

Part 1. PARISH AFFAIRS

1. Diocesan quota   £...............
2. Clergy expenses of office   ....
3. Maintenance of fabric   ....
4. Heating and lighting of church and hall   ....
5. Wages-organist, cleaner, choir boys and
   girls, parish secretary   ....
6. Insurance   ....
7. Sunday School and Youth Work   ....
8. Miscellaneous items   ....

Total of Part 1   £

Part 2. OUTSIDE THE PARISH

1. Support for the work of the Church
   overseas   ....
2. Support for the Cathedral   ....
3. Giving to other good causes   ....
                                                 ─────────

Total of Part 2   £
                                                 ─────────

Some careful thought will need to be given to every item. Some will think that some things are not really very important and maybe not at all necessary. The most contentious area may well be that of outside giving, since most have their favourite charities. People might be encouraged to give some of their income not to the Church but direct to those charities. As a rough rule it might be decided that the PCC should support worthy causes that are unlikely to attract much support from the non-church-going public. This might mean an annual contribution to the Friends of the Cathedral, since visitors to cathedrals are not noted for the generosity of their gifts.

(5) *Deed of Covenant Schemes*

Signing deeds of covenant should be an integral part of any stewardship campaign. In this country it is the policy of the government to permit charities to reclaim from the Inland Revenue the tax already paid on covenanted sums. I sometimes wonder if the Americans do things better than we do. In their country it is, I believe, the practice that covenanted contributions to charity (including of course the Church) are allowable for tax relief. Their plan seems to be that the tax relief benefits the donor while ours benefits the charity. Presumably it all comes to the same thing in the long run.

People seem to have a thing about signing a covenant, but if they pay income tax there are no snags at all. A covenant made by somebody paying tax at 30 per cent means that for every £1 you give, the Church gets 43p extra. It has to be for a minimum of four years. If you pay higher tax than 30 per cent the Church benefits even more. A covenant can always be transferred from one church to another, if for example you move. Many of us find it amazing that tax-paying Church members who give generously and regularly refuse to sign a covenant, a simple government-approved method of giving additional help to charity at no extra cost whatsoever to the donor. Those who want the fullest details should refer to *Covenants* by Michael Norton (Directory of Social Change, 1982). It is a very sound practical guide. Model forms of deeds of covenant and also a booklet *Deeds of Covenant: Notes for Officers of Parochial Church Councils* are available from the Church House Bookshop.

(6) *Special Appeals*

A great many parishes suddenly have to find a vast sum of money for essential repairs to the church or the organ which is beyond the capacity of the fabric fund. A special appeal is then necessary, so when stewardship campaigns take place, it is advisable not to give an undertaking that you will make no further demands for money.

First of all a restoration committee should be appointed. The chairman is the key figure and people with drive and ideas should be asked to serve on it. The PCC will decide what amount it can pay into the restoration fund to start it off; then the appeal will be launched. At a very early stage the restoration committee will have to decide if the appeal should be confined to church members or beamed at the whole local community. You should bear in mind it is not only the regular worshippers who value the church building; people who rarely come regard it as their church and would be the first to protest if anyone suggested that it might close down.

Prayer support is vital. The project should be prayed for

publicly at all services, that all decisions made should be in accordance with God's will. The regular daily prayers of all members of the congregation should be asked for and a suitably printed prayer card could be printed and widely distributed. Regular thanksgivings should also be offered as the appeal proceeds. One diocesan bishop told me that he had never known a parish appeal that had been carefully prayed about at every stage to do anything other than succeed.

Prayer is never meant to be a substitute for hard work, and imaginative fund-raising events will be needed. The usual sales of work and garden fêtes and wine-and-cheese evenings will have a new sense of urgency. A talent scheme is valuable, when you give out one pound notes to as many as will take them, giving them a year to increase this sum by any means they think fit. A Festival of Flowers is an inspiration in itself. When it is coupled with the restoration appeal it can be even more effective and bring in large sums of money.

The diocese will often help. Most boards of finance will give both a grant and an interest-free loan to start a scheme off. Local authorities can make cash grants for this purpose if they so desire and many do. Interest free loans from church members are also most useful and these may enable a contract to be placed more quickly. The PCC should resolve to pay back all such loans within, say, five years.

The launching and carrying out of a massive restoration project can be a very exhilarating experience but it is also very time-consuming for the incumbent. He may query whether he was really ordained to be a fund-raiser, but if he refuses to take any interest in an appeal, it will probably fail.

An astonishing variety of money-raising schemes will be found in *Fund Raising A to Z* by Alan Robinson (Kirkfield Publications, 1982)

(7) *Fees*

A small but significant contribution to parish finances comes from fees. Parochial Fees orders are issued from time to time by the Church Commissioners and copies can be obtained from 1 Millbank, London SW1P 3JZ. An odd feature of the 1983 Order states the amount of 'the fee payable to the incumbent as part of his stipend' but surely it is generally known that in fact no fees are retained by any incumbent for his own use. All have to be declared and are subtracted from his stipend augmentation. Some regard this as unfair and unfortunate because some incumbents may have literally hundreds of baptisms, weddings and funerals annually and others scarcely any. But there appears to be no satisfactory answer to this anomaly.

The Order makes it clear that no fees may be charged for a baptism, only for a baptism certificate. It also makes it clear that the fees quoted do not include charges for music, bells, flowers or special heating. These will be decided by the incumbent and PCC. Quite large fees are payable to the PCC for marriages, funerals, burials, monuments in the church-yard and searches in church registers, and some feel they are, on the whole, too large. Some feel they would like to see all fees abolished and everything laid on free of charge.

But the plain fact is that the Church needs the money and there is no evidence that the existing fees are at all off-putting. It should be understood that vast sums are paid for weddings and funerals, often running into many hundreds of pounds. Surely nobody resents the comparatively modest sums paid to the Church.

I well recall, during a debate about fees in General Synod, somebody raising the point that in some cases the incumbent (and he alone) ought to have the right to remit all or part of the fees in particular cases of need. He was told that this would reduce the amount received by the diocese towards clergy stipends; but I strongly suspect that some incumbents still remit all or part of the fees when they possess confidential information that suggests this is the right thing to do. Many of us would strongly deplore any efforts made to remove this freedom.

Chapter 6

The Parish Secretary

(1) *The Parish Office*

When the original professional fund-raising companies operated in parishes of every type and in every diocese, they greatly surprised us by demanding—and getting—office facilities of a far higher standard than anything previously considered appropriate. Even in the poorest parish the organizer insisted on a parish office of some kind, complete with telephone, typewriter, duplicator and adding machine; and he required the services of a full-time shorthand typist.

A number of parishes decided to retain the parish office after the campaign was over and to continue to employ at least a part-time secretary, to continue the high standards of efficiency, to keep careful records of the planned giving contributions and to free the incumbent for other more important tasks that only he could perform. Of course, the increased income resulting from the campaign affected the decision; parishes running on a shoe-string cannot possibly find the extra money required.

The cost of setting up a parish office is considerable but there is no doubt that it is money well spent. It is best to have office and study fairly close to each other because there is a fair amount of coming and going between secretary and incumbent, ideally two adjoining rooms. Some maintain that these rooms should be in the church or hall so that the parsonage house can be the home of the parish priest and his family, a home that he and they can enjoy without interruption from constant callers. Others of us feel strongly that in most parishes this is a mistaken view; our homes cannot possibly be islands if the parish is alive. Where this is not possible, a study in the house and an office in the church can be made to work well if the two are not a great distance apart.

Of course we know that it is diocesan policy to dispose of vast old Georgian and Victorian parsonage houses that used to be such familiar features of the parochial scene, replacing them with small modern houses, usually purpose-built. These include a study with perhaps a separate entrance door so that callers can knock on the study door itself and not disturb the vicarage family. What a splendid thing it would be if a small outer office for the secretary could be included.

(2) *Office Equipment*

For all too long it has been taken for granted that the incumbent's office equipment must be supplied by himself and paid for and maintained at his own expense. Now many a flourishing parish sees to it that the equipment is just as good as the parish can afford, knowing that this approach makes for far greater efficiency, far less worry, and work of the highest standard. Incidentally it also may well mean that maintenance charges on new items will be very substantially less than those for old and rather worn equipment, an important item with maintenance charges so very high.

A good electric typewriter with 16-inch carriage is the most important item. The idea of this is to take A4 size paper and stencils longways on. My stationer tells me that foolscap-size paper is still in great demand (13×8 inches) and the smaller quarto, but obviously the move is to A4 and A5, and as A4 size is approximately $11\frac{3}{4} \times 8\frac{1}{4}$ inches and A5 half this, it will not make the slightest difference to one's office work to change over and be up-to-date. The cost of an electric typewriter? I saw Smith-Corona ones advertised for £100 in 1983 and the larger and more elaborate office models £300. The golf-ball kind will cost more. Secondly, a good electric duplicator is a must. Roneo and Gestetner are the big names here but there are others. The important thing is to ensure that good back-up facilities are available, so that if the machine is not working well it can be promptly put right. It is possible to buy factory rebuilt models and good second-hand models should not be ruled out.

A special telephone installation is essential. The old plan 107 used to be ideal but this has been replaced by what is known as the Ambassador Electronic Switching System, something far more elaborate but, oddly enough, rather cheaper in quarterly rental than its predecessor. The main instrument is placed in the parish office and the extension in your study (it can always be put through direct when the secretary is not on duty). If you have any need for them, two more extensions are possible. The Ambassador is for 'a small business or office that needs internal as well as external communications'—just what we need! It is a modern micro-processor controlled system but that need not put anybody off. With it, you can call your secretary or she you by pressing a button—and of course all such calls are free of charge. All incoming calls can come to the secretary and she can get the outgoing ones. It should cost about £50 to install and about £1.50 for quarterly charge.

One priest told me that one of the best things he ever did was to acquire a telephone answering machine. He had no secretary but held, as do most Roman Catholic parish priests, that the plant ought always to be manned in case of emergencies. Anybody who calls when you are out can leave a message which you play back immediately you get in. The cost might be £125, but I can well believe that it is a valuable asset.

There are of course numerous other items. A good filing

cabinet that can be locked is vital. A copying machine—the kind of thing that photographs instantaneously any paper you care to insert—is surely very useful indeed. I have never had one because I have always been lucky enough to have ready access to ones possessed by others; but those who have them tell me how useful they are.

There is another item that is essential—a dictating machine. It seems that shorthand is on the way out and many an experienced secretary no longer uses this skill. Younger women probably never had it, for audio-typing is now acceptable in every major office and personal dictation no longer general. If you are lucky enough to find somebody who can do shorthand, that is fine, but you still need the dictating machine if you are to make good use of your secretary. You will find two pieces of equipment are best, one being a small hand-held affair into which you can dictate and the other a desk machine which is complete with microphone, footswitch and earphones. The cost? We are probably talking about £300 or more for new equipment, but there are second-hand ones that cost far less.

All this equipment is so expensive that your first instinct may well be: 'The parish could never run to anything like this'. But the parish will if it is large and lively and supportive and longs to see efficient, superbly-produced matter coming out of the parish office, that is at least as good as the sort of thing leading members of the congregation take for granted in their own offices. And this is really my plea. It is for high standards of work. Surely we have outgrown the period when people automatically expected everything connected with their parish church to be sordid, shabby and unworthy.

Careful thought should be given to taking advantage of the Churches Purchasing Scheme, whereby often very large discounts can be obtained on practically everything you are likely to require. The various discounts have been negotiated by the Central Board of Finance and full details can be obtained from Church House, Dean's Yard, Westminster SW1P 3NZ. I have the current catalogue open in front of me and it is clear that not only major items of equipment but even stencils and paper can be obtained more cheaply than locally. Some prefer to deal locally and pay more, partly to support the local man and partly to be sure of prompt back-up service if anything goes wrong.

Many years ago I wrote an article that appeared in the *Church Times* advocating the employment of parish secretaries and stressing the need for top-quality equipment and general high standards. It provoked some interesting, disapproving letters suggesting that what I was recommending was an unwarrantable extravagance and quite unnecessary. Now countless parishes have them. With the number of full-time parish priests still declining it is surely obvious that, far from being an extravagance, parish secretaries relieve many a parish priest of routine chores, enabling him to get on with the job for which he was ordained.

(3) *The Secretary*

The choosing of the secretary is important, for she becomes very much a key figure in the running of the parish. She must be competent, reliable and of course absolutely discreet. She will get to know about highly confidential matters. Some think it best to appoint as secretary somebody who is neither a parishioner nor a member of the congregation just because of this need for confidentiality; but I don't know that this is all-important provided you are sure of her discretion. I once had a pillar of the congregation as parish secretary and there was never any question of a single confidence being betrayed.

She ought to be paid because she is a professional. Many a woman who was previously a top secretary has married and has had children; but as the children grow older she may long for a part-time, thoroughly interesting job, that can be made to fit in with her duties as wife and mother and that will enable her to employ the skills she has acquired professionally. Each time I advertised for a secretary I had a minor avalanche of replies from just this sort of person.

My secretary used to come from 9.30 a.m.–12 noon from Mondays to Fridays. If she wanted a day off (perhaps because of a school occasion) she could always have it—and make up for it by staying longer another day. She worked for me for about $12\frac{1}{2}$ hours weekly and *if* the agreed rate was £2 an hour this would work out at about £25 a week.

This would be beyond the reach of many a parish, as would the costly items of equipment previously mentioned. But here is an interesting thing. In one of the poorer parishes in which I served, where this sort of thing was clearly out of the question, I had three competent women, two with previous secretarial experience and one still so engaged, who volunteered to come and help me for nothing. They saw the job as comparable to running the refreshments at a social or organizing youth activities or any other of the countless voluntary jobs that are done in a parish. I used all three. We acquired cheap, second-hand equipment and the three produced work of at least reasonable standard and were of tremendous help to me. But I strongly hold that a paid professional is better. She may be perfectly happy with a much lower wage than the going rate, particularly if her husband earns good money. She does it because the job is so interesting, so absorbing and so important. One secretary I had who came under precisely these conditions stayed for ten years.

(4) *The Secretary's Duties*

If the office is in the house she can deal tactfully with callers and answer the telephone. Her first job every morning should be letters. The busier we are in our parishes, the more letters we get and the less time we have to deal with them. As you can dictate perhaps a dozen letters in little over half an hour, there is no excuse for failing to answer promptly; moreover, the letters will be beautifully typed and copies of them can be filed.

In my last parish we had a very efficient secretary. We were able to duplicate and circulate (free of charge) well over 400 copies of a weekly newsletter every week. They were handed out to members of each congregation as they came in and made giving out of notices unnecessary. The newsletter is not a substitute for the parish magazine, but more of that later. I found it best to dictate the newsletter on Friday mornings, and the job took the secretary the whole of that morning. Mine had shorthand, but I could equally well have dictated it to the dictating machine. The cost of the weekly newsletter would be that of a ream of A5 paper and a couple of stencils.

She will also be able to type and duplicate agendas and minutes of the PCC and finance committees, the monthly music lists and the parish magazine. She can duplicate tickets for social functions instead of your having them printed. It is possible to duplicate the accounts as well as the ballot papers for the annual parochial church meeting. The secretary can do all sorts of jobs for the various organizations in the parish such as printing the annual programme of events, rotas of all kinds and duty lists for every organization that needs them. As printing becomes steadily more expensive the economy of duplicating is a very useful one.

(5) *Full-Time Duties*

It is unreasonable to expect a part-time secretary to do much more than I have described. It would certainly be a gain for any parish to have a full-time secretary but only the very large and very busy parishes would be likely to be able to afford this. Those that do probably expect her to record the planned giving, look after the incumbent's filing system, keep his diary, remind him of engagements, prepare his lists of visits and keep up to date his card-index of people visited by entering all the appropriate details. In many parishes a substantial number of parishioners are on the telephone. The secretary can ring up people in advance of the vicar's proposed visit and save much time. People still appreciate a visit from the parish priest and are sorry if they happen to be out when he calls.

There is one other advantage: many a Roman Catholic priest would regard it as a tremendous condemnation of his ministry if somebody phoned him at any hour and was unable to get any reply; whilst I think this view a little extreme, it would be valuable to have somebody to take messages, especially during the day.

Incidentally, the parish secretary takes her orders only from the incumbent but she is employed by the parish, not him. I was always a little put out when asked to include her wages as part of my expenses paid by the parish for me. This must surely be wrong. Is the pay of, say, the verger to be so regarded? He does countless things for the incumbent but I have never heard it suggested that he should be included on the incumbent's expense sheet. The verger, the organist and the secretary are all employed by the parish for the parish. Each of them helps the incumbent in many different ways and all take their orders from him and from nobody else. But not one of them should be regarded as part of the incumbent's expenses of office.

Chapter 7

The Parish Services

(1) *Endless Variety*

'Now from henceforth', wrote Cranmer in the preface to *The Book of Common Prayer*, 'all the whole realm shall have but one use.' It has not worked out like that. Few parish priests in the twentieth century have stuck rigidly to the 1662 forms but many have made only minor alterations. Some introduced forms based on Roman Catholic usage. For the great majority of us, many of the forms printed in the 1928 Prayer Book found favour, notably the services of Holy Baptism, Holy Matrimony and Christian Burial. Parts of the 1928 Holy Communion service and the variations in Morning Prayer and Evening Prayer became very common. The result was that no two parishes were the same. A family, having got used to one set of services, might move away to another parish—and find something quite different. This was one of the many concerns of the Liturgical Commission. Would they be able to produce one book that everybody, no matter of what churchmanship, would be able and willing to use?

(2) *The Alternative Service Book 1980*

In 1965 the Prayer Book (Alternative and Other Services) Measure was passed and the Liturgical Commission soon began to produce many forms of service alternative to those in the *Book of Common Prayer*. The procedure was slow and cumbersome and I well recall the seemingly endless debates in General Synod, when we ran through each service virtually line by line. The Liturgical Commission gave the impression that they actually welcomed revisions sketched out on the back of an envelope on the spur of the moment by members. Several really were put forward in that way and carried. The great problem soon became very apparent. Would it ever be possible to satisfy conservative Evangelicals on the one hand and uncompromising Anglo Catholics on the other?

For years we had to put up with little books—Series 1, Series 2, Series 3, even Series 1 and 2 combined. It was all very confusing. But at long last the great day came when *The Alternative Service Book 1980* was published. It was just fifteen years after the passing of the Prayer Book (Alternative and Other Services) Measure was passed. It was a great day for the then chairman of the Commission, Canon Ronald Jasper, whose seemingly endless patience impressed us all.

It contained just about everything except forms of *Ministry to The Sick* (this duly appeared in 1983). Very soon sales exceeded expectations and by the end of 1983 they were over 800,000 for the full pew edition. The sales of 'separates' were tremendous and continue to be very satisfactory. Many parishes obtained permission to print their own Holy Communion booklets.

An invaluable book appeared in 1980 that ought to be compulsory reading for all incumbents. It is called *The Alternative Service Book 1980—A Commentary by the Liturgical Commission*, published by the Church Information Office. This commentary was produced in the light of its experience in compiling the services and explains why things were done, the objects of it all and the ways in which the book ought to be used. It indicates how the services were modified in the light of experimental use. There is a splendid chapter on the background of the ASB, tracing the steps that led up to its acceptance, but the most valuable feature is a detailed commentary on each of the new services.

What is happening is this. Almost every parish has given careful consideration to the matter of using the new book, whether all the services or just some of them. The decision must be a joint one by the minister and the PCC (Canon B3.1). A new incumbent cannot change the use agreed by the PCC and his predecessor. It must always be by agreement. But with the occasional offices it is the minister who conducts the service who decides which form to use unless any of the people concerned objects (Canon B3.4).

Parish after parish has changed to the ASB for Holy Communion. The new lectionary is generally used and many parishes make use of the new provision that allows the Holy Communion readings to be used at Morning or Evening Prayer. Many a parish priest has more than one church and this sensible provision makes it unnecessary to compose several sermons when one will do for all. The new Holy Communion services are either Rite A or Rite B. Rite A is the one that addresses the deity as 'you', while Rite B is the conservative one that continues 'thee' and 'thou'. Both are very flexible and allow many variations; we are still a very long way from the Cranmer ideal.

Parishes that decide to use the ASB must make an important decision—to buy copies for everybody (obviously involving the expenditure of a large sum of money), or to obtain separates or to have their own booklets printed. I suspect that most of us got very tired of the little booklets we had to use for so many years. They got tattier and tattier. It is obviously best to have the whole book so that people can follow the readings. Some parishes invite parishioners to give one or more new books, perhaps in memory of somebody. Some buy just a few for visitors and encourage regulars to buy and bring their own. A generous discount scheme is available to those parishes that decide to order in bulk (less 20 per cent on fifty copies or more).

It should be understood that General Synod never meant

The Book of Common Prayer to be quietly phased out. This superb work will always be lawful. It is often used perhaps at 8 a.m. Sunday celebrations of Holy Communion and on weekdays and it is probably more popular than the ASB at Mattins and Evensong. Inevitably there are some vociferous Anglicans who make the most extraordinary claims for it, claiming that the changeover to the ASB is responsible for a general falling-off in church attendance and that huge numbers would come to church if, and only if, *The Book of Common Prayer* was used. Every parish priest knows this claim to be totally unfounded.

(3) *Which Service?*

I well recall back in the fifties hearing Dr Frank Lake, founder of the Clinical Theology Association, addressing a gathering of clergy in Bristol. This is how he began: 'Gentlemen, in your parishes you have your 8 a.m. Holy Communion congregations. These are your schizophrenics. These worshippers hate other people. They like to come by themselves, sit by themselves (preferably behind a column) and be left alone. Don't try to talk to them before or after the service. They just want to be left alone. Then you have your 11 a.m. Mattins congregations. These are your neurotic compulsives. They hate change. They want things to be just as they have always known them. Be careful of these people, gentlemen, for they are the geese that lay the golden eggs, your most generous givers. Then you have your 6 p.m. Evensong congregations. These are your manic depressives. They hate themselves. They come to be cheered up. Have only well-known hymns. Crack a joke or two in your sermon. Shake every hand at the church door. Gentlemen, as I see it, your principal problem is find how to weld these three strands into a single Parish Communion.'

This penetrating analysis showed rare perception, although it has to be said that Dr Lake upset a great many of his hearers. In spite of his strictures, the 8 a.m. Holy

Communion is likely to continue. Some really do like the peace and quiet of it and tend to come to no other service. This means they may never hear a sermon. But the ASB is quite firm that 'The Sermon is an integral part of the Ministry of the Word. A sermon should normally be preached at all celebrations on Sundays and other Holy Days'. But it need not be anything other than short. There is a useful book called *Introductions to the ASB Readings* by William Collins (Mowbray, 1982) and these might be read as a sermon substitute. In *Reflections on the Readings for Holy Communion* by Dennis Page (Mowbray, 1983) there are some rather longer expositions and these would serve admirably.

Sunday Mattins is also likely to continue. It was Cranmer who reduced from seven to two the normal daily round of offices, which consisted of the reciting of psalms, the reading of two Bible passages and the saying of prayers. This form of service was based upon that used by our Lord himself every Sabbath day in the synagogue. Cranmer meant Mattins to be a preparation for Holy Communion, but in Victorian times it became the chief Sunday service and it has remained so in many a parish.

At Mattins there is time to develop a theme in a sermon and twenty minutes or more is common and indeed expected. Strangers coming to this service can follow everything, unlike the Eucharist. It appeals more than any other service to a great many elderly people and where Mattins is presented with dignity and imagination it holds the loyalty of often large numbers. It would be foolish and thoughtless for a new incumbent who found a flourishing Mattins tradition to drop it and replace it with some other service.

Sunday Evensong used to be the most popular service of all. In the East London parish where I served my title an Evensong congregation of 500 or more was usual. Now many a parish finds great difficulty in attracting even a tiny congregation. Television is a formidable counter-attraction (*Sunday Half-Hour* clashes with the normal Evensong time). But some parishes, those with fine choirs for instance, attract large evening congregations still. Sometimes there is a flourishing Youth Club that meets on Sunday evenings, and the members may play a conspicuous part in presenting the service.

One of the worries about Mattins and Evensong is the fact that children and young people are so conspicuous by their absence. Somehow neither service, just as it is, either in *The Book of Common Prayer* or the ASB, seems to attract them. Many parishes, aware of this fact, have a Families' Service on Sunday mornings. True, no provision for such services is made either in the ASB or in the Canons but, provided the statutory services are held, there is no objection to additional services, as is made clear by Canon B5.2. The statutory services are Morning and Evening Prayer and Holy Communion but the Bishop may authorize certain dispensations (Canon B11.2). Obviously, where you have one parish priest serving several parishes much flexibility is called for.

Families' Services are beamed chiefly at young children up to the age of twelve or so and the idea is to attract them with their parents. I know of many such services that are most successful in attracting very large numbers every Sunday. The form of service can be drawn up by the parish priest, often with the help of others. The children must have plenty to do and plenty to look at. An overhead screen is a great help (the cost of a suitable projector might be about £120) and some of the clergy are highly skilled in using them. Children should read the lessons, take the prayers, act as churchwardens, take the collection and so on. Often they take part in dances or mimes or playlets. Children love these services and so do their parents.

Obviously much careful thought must be given to the ordering of services on Sundays and involving people in worship. Many would say that this surely must be our top priority, our main concern. The worship of almighty God must come before all else.

(4) *The Parish Communion*

It seems reasonably clear that Mattins is declining in popularity and Families' Services are not always held every Sunday. Churches which have the latter every Sunday often attract very large congregations to them and it is certainly a wonderful experience to take part in what are always joyful and inspiring occasions. It is lovely to see so many eager young faces and one feels that good seed is certainly being sown. But there is one great worry. The children tend to stay away well before the age of twelve. The service is seen by them to be what indeed it is, i.e. kids' stuff. If the hope is that such children will move on naturally to Mattins then great disappointment is likely to result. The children find Mattins boring. They simply fall away—and so do the parents.

The Parish Communion does not have this weakness. It has been most exciting to see it steadily gain in popularity. Dr Frank Lake was right in seeing the size of the problem all those years ago. Now I imagine that quite three-quarters of all parishes, high and low included, make this the central service of the day. The ASB has greatly helped to provide a motive for change. The PCC and incumbent together decide whether to make it Rite A or Rite B, and many a parish has a worship committee that decides, with the incumbent, which variations are best. Often several things are tried before a decision is made.

What is the best time? It seems to me that 10 a.m. is ideal. On the one hand, the children can be got ready and brought along. On the other, mum gets home in good time to get the Sunday lunch, still the most significant family event of the week in countless homes. I would hate to have my main service at a time when children could not possibly attend or at a time that led to the dropping of the hot roast meal. This may be the one meal of the week where the whole family, including of course dad, sit down for a leisurely occasion where talk really does occur.

There are those who say the Parish Communion is not the

answer to all our problems. Of course it isn't. The real problem is making any impact upon a largely semi-pagan population. Some of us think this service is most likely to make at least a slight impact. Of course, the service has to be carefully and painstakingly built up. Everything in the parish leads up to it and away from it. This is the service where uniformed youth organizations parade and where new choir members are enrolled. This is where new Mothers' Union members are admitted. This is the one to which visiting preachers are invited. There are all sorts of ways of making it clear, both in teaching and preaching, that this is **the** great weekly family gathering—and it is marred if anybody is missing. One incumbent known to me insisted on the names of anybody missing being brought up at the weekly staff meeting, and he arranged for every one to be visited to find out why! This is the service at which banns are published, the sick prayed for by name and the departed commended. It must be made crystal clear that this is **the** family service, **the** weekly family gathering, **the** most important event of the week.

Arrangements must be made to meet the needs of whole families. A creche for babies is vital (for children up to say three years) and a graded Sunday school ought to run in parallel. More is said about this later.

At the ASB services of Holy Communion we note that the emphasis is carefully placed on both the ministry of the word and the sacrament. It is clear that lay people are meant to be involved, to participate, to share responsibility—and not just to attend. I am a great believer in involving as many people as one possibly can. There are of course choir members, bell ringers, sidesmen, churchwardens and servers. There can and ought to be lesson readers, people taking part in the offertory procession, chalice administrators and (occasionally) a member of the congregation preaching the sermon. It is a curious thing that in some parishes the feeling still seems to be that these things are good but only if done by men. Does anybody now take seriously St Paul's injunction that women ought to keep silent in church? There is another curious impression that only an ordained clergyman can read the gospel for the day or administer the paten. This is not what Canon Law lays down. Canon B12.4 makes it clear that both the epistle and the gospel may be read by a lay person at the invitation of the minister while Canon B12.3 makes it clear that persons can be authorized by the bishop 'to distribute the holy sacrament'. 'Person' is meant to cover both men and women. The usual procedure for administrators is for names to be brought by the incumbent to the PCC for approval before submission to the bishop.

I thankfully record that I have known women church-wardens, women/sidesmen, women administrators, women lesson readers, girl servers, and women leading the intercessions. All did the job at least as well as men.

(5) *The Peace and the Agape*

If you want your congregation to become a family in any meaningful sense then careful attention should be paid to the Peace and to the modern equivalent of the *Agape*. In the ASB, after the Peace the rubric says that the president may say 'Let us offer one another a sign of peace'. Anglicans are traditionally supposed to be unfriendly compared with members of the Free Churches and often it is quite difficult to persuade worshippers to do anything of the sort. In one parish I found great difficulty in persuading people to shake hands and say something like 'Peace to you' to somebody not a member of their own family until one totally blind woman who came every Sunday said to me: 'I can't tell you how wonderful I find the Peace. Every Sunday somebody touches me, putting a hand on my shoulder or clasping my hand. It is the making of my week. When I made this public there were no further objections. Sometimes the Peace is very elaborately observed. In one church I know everybody has a word with every other member of the congregation, with much kissing and embracing. Some of us find all that too much. Probably it is best for the whole thing to take less than one minute, with everybody being urged to exchange a sign of peace with somebody they do not know well.

I used to urge people to bring into the church hall for coffee any newcomer they exchanged the Peace with. The coffee session in the hall afterwards (or even in church if the hall is unsuitable or too far away) is vitally important. Eucharist is meant to be followed by *Agape* and the old idea of going quietly home is definitely out. Of course, worshippers must be urged not to speak just to their own friends and neighbours but to look out for somebody they do not know well. I used to ask newcomers who came into the hall how many people had spoken to them—and if the answer was nobody I would have something to say in church the following Sunday! This social gathering is good. By the way, talking to people afterwards is surely right, just as talking before the service is not helpful to those who come in good time to prepare themselves. I often used to print in the newsletter in bold type: 'Be thoughtful, be silent, be reverent, for this is the house of God. Before the service, speak to the Lord; during the service, let the Lord speak to you; after the service, speak to one another.'

Observance of the Peace and the *Agape* seems to ensure steady growth in numbers. I have seen it happen time and again, and here is a curious fact. There seems to be no very great difficulty in a town parish in reaching somewhere around 200 communicants at Parish Communion but there seems to be a sort of 'sound barrier' at that point that is difficult to break through. The reason is probably the time taken for administration. People do not have the spiritual resources for a long period. Careful thought should be given to ways of ensuring that the time taken for the administration is not greater than the time taken for the sermon, otherwise the balance of the service is ruined. A good many administrators, as many as are needed, helps. There can be numerous administration points, not necessarily at an altar and not necessarily involving kneeling. We should think and plan in terms of much larger numbers—and these larger numbers are likely to come if the congregation is friendly and welcoming.

(6) *House Communions*

Ernest Southcott, when he was Vicar of Halton, Yorks, first experimented with house communions. He told the story in *The Parish Comes Alive* (Mowbray, 1956). Since then the idea has developed as a valuable extension of God's kingdom and in many parishes house groups are very common. A group that has met regularly for prayer, discussion, instruction or fellowship may feel that it would like a house communion service. The conduct of the service should be as simple as possible: the priest will probably, but not necessarily, wear cassock and surplice; communicants will stand around the table; ordinary bread will be used. Celebrations will take place in the evening, when all can be present, and there is no objection to ordinary working clothes being worn. The permission of the bishop will be needed before celebrating Holy Communion in a private house. In parishes where large numbers of electoral roll members are non-resident and where a group meets in a house in another parish, a house communion should be held only with the goodwill of the incumbent concerned. On no account must the house communion be regarded as a substitute for or an alternative to the Sunday Eucharist in the parish church and this means that they should be occasional rather than frequent. Communicant members of other churches should be invited to join in. Unconfirmed Anglicans should be encouraged to attend but not to communicate unless they mean to be confirmed in due course. Nobody can doubt the great value of house communions.

(7) *Decently and in Order*

Conducting church services is one of our most important duties. L. S. Hunter in *A Parson's Job* (1931) puts it even more strongly: 'Everything that a minister of religion may be called upon to do is subordinate to the function of leading a congregation in worship'. We should surely act as though it is. It is important to get to church at least fifteen minutes before the service is timed to begin. Everything must be ready in good time. The church should be spotless, altar linen should be immaculate, books should be in a good state of repair, notice-boards should be up to date and a high standard of tidiness should be achieved. Every service should start punctually. If the incumbent sets a bad example in any of these things it will not be long before everybody else ceases to bother very much either. Everybody should know exactly what to do. This is important not only at routine services but also on special occasions. On special occasions a careful rehearsal of all taking a leading part is vital, so that everything goes smoothly on the day.

We have to teach our people to be reverent, to regard the services as vitally important, and to see them as a weekly duty and privilege. We are not likely to succeed in this task unless everything is done decently and in order.

Chapter 8

Parish Communication

(1) *The Need*

Much of the work of a parish priest lies in the field of communication. He has the gospel to proclaim, and the Bible to teach; he has a duty to guide the thoughts of his parishioners on the great moral issues of the day. He has to communicate to the congregation in church. In addition, he has to communicate to children (in a church school perhaps or Sunday school), to his confirmation candidates and the youth club; he must also communicate to specialized groups such as CEMS, MU or perhaps neighbourhood groups and the older, less active people who may be housebound but who nevertheless want to maintain contact with the life of their parish church.

Finally, the incumbent must lead the parish in its vital mission to others inside the parish boundaries but outside the church, projecting the image of a vital church, a caring church to all who will listen.

(2) *The Sermon*

His first vehicle of communication must be the sermon. The sermon is regarded as unimportant by some parish priests, notably those who are content with just a few words from the chancel step at Parish Communion. Thankfully, the place of the sermon is now becoming widely recognized. It is of course nonsense to claim that only a few words are required at Parish Communion. There is no reason why ten minutes should be regarded as the maximum length; this can certainly be exceeded if circumstances demand it. It should not be supposed that everybody is desperately anxious to be out of church in less than one hour! The importance of the sermon is stressed in *The Ministry of the Word* by D. W. Cleverley Ford (Hodder and Stoughton, 1979) and *I Believe in Preaching* by John Stott (Hodder and Stoughton, 1982). Both authors believe preaching to be as important as ever and Dr Cleverley Ford has done an immense amount to re-establish the place of the sermon. I have reviewed no less than fourteen books of sermons in recent years, clear evidence that a demand exists. All of us can learn much from the masters.

In 1978 the Church of England adopted a new two-year table of lessons for use at Communion services, each Sunday having two sets of three readings, used in alternative years. They are printed in full in the ASB and are taken from various versions of the Bible. The versions authorized under the Versions of the Bible Measure 1965 are the Authorized Version, the Revised Version, the Revised Standard Version, the New English Bible, the Jerusalem Bible and Today's English Version (the Good News Bible). Each is used in the ASB, the ideas determining the choice being 'accuracy of translation, simplicity, clarity, the requirements of public as opposed to private reading, and the need for a version which is not at variance with the language of the ASB' (*Commentary by the Liturgical Commission*). The Communion readings may be used if required at Morning and Evening Prayer, thus providing for the clergyman who has to minister to several congregations at different services. Full provision is also made for two other readings for Morning and Evening Prayer. Where the Communion readings are used it should be noted that every Sunday has a special theme (ASB p. 1092).

More and more churches are tending to stick to the suggested theme, which is meant to link the readings, the sermon, the hymns and the prayers. Several books are available to help us to come to grips with these themes. I have listed some in the bibliography.

There is a lot to be said for using Advent and Lent and the Sundays after Easter for special courses of sermons. For Advent the traditional Four Last Things can be considered—Death, Judgement, Hell and Heaven. Lent is quite the best season for courses, not least because a great many people still regard Lent as a time for self-denial, for greater effort, for fasting and discipline. Much depends upon the incumbent. If a parish makes much of Lent there may be considerable interest in such courses and they may attract larger than usual congregations.

Imaginative titles for courses of sermons help. Here are some suggestions that may be found useful:

THE SEVEN DEADLY SINS
1. Pride
2. Anger
3. Lust
4. Envy and Avarice
5. Gluttony
6. Sloth

MAKING ALL THINGS NEW
1. New Sorrow
2. New Life
3. New Prayer
4. New Sight
5. A New Attitude
6. A New Faith

BEING A CHRISTIAN INVOLVES:
1. Worship
2. Telling Others

3. Caring for Others
4. Duties at Home
5. Understanding the Faith
6. Giving

THE CREED
1. I Believe in God the Father Almighty
2. I Believe in Jesus Christ
3. I Believe in the Holy Spirit
4. I Believe in One Holy Catholic Apostolic Church
5. I Believe in the Communion of Saints
6. I Believe in the Forgiveness of Sins

THE SIX ROADS TO HEAVEN
1. Except a man be born again . . .
2. Except ye repent . . .
3. Except ye be converted . . .
4. Except your righteousness exceed . . .
5. Except ye eat the flesh . . .
6. Except a corn of wheat . . .

SQUARE WORDS IN A ROUND WORLD
1. Incarnation
2. Atonement
3. Trinitarianism
4. Grace
5. Crucifixion
6. Resurrection

POPULAR HYMNS AND THEIR MEANING
1. Forty days and forty nights
2. The Church's one foundation
3. Rock of ages
4. Jesu, Lover of my soul
5. There is a green hill far away
6. When I survey the wondrous cross

TALKING POINTS
1. Fasting—is it out of date?
2. Sexual standards—are there now new ones?
3. Pacifism—are all wars wrong?
4. Britain—is patriotism a vice or virtue?
5. Prayer—does it work?
6. Death—ought a dying person to be told?

SOME OLD TESTAMENT PERSONALITIES
1. Dictatorship without Tyranny—Moses
2. Brawn without Brains—Samson
3. Obedience without Question—Samuel
4. Forgiveness without Reserve—David
5. Courage without Arrogance—Elijah
6. Disaster without Despair—Jeremiah

THE SACRAMENTS
1. What are sacraments?
2. Baptism—Man's Part
3. Baptism—God's Part
4. Confirmation
5. Holy Communion—Man's Part
6. Holy Communion—God's Part

JUST A WORD
1. Come
2. Give
3. Watch
4. Learn
5. Go
6. Do

WHAT CHRISTIANITY HAS TO SAY ABOUT:
1. Peace and War
2. Marriage
3. Work
4. Leisure

5. Suffering
6. Death

I BELIEVE IN GOD
1. God our Creator
2. God our Father
3. God our Lord
4. God our Redeemer
5. God our Peace
6. God our Hope

THE 'I AM'S' OF JESUS
1. Before Abraham was, I am
2. I am the Bread of Life
3. I am the Light of the World
4. I am the Door
5. I am the Good Shepherd
6. I am the Resurrection and the Life

SIX GREAT OLD TESTAMENT LOVERS
1. Adam, who loved his wife
2. Joseph, who loved his brothers
3. Moses, who loved the law
4. David, who loved his armies
5. Solomon, who loved his court
6. Elijah, who loved his God

(3) *Visiting Preachers*

Sometimes a course by visiting preachers can be very
stimulating. They may be local clergy or perhaps well known
laymen whose views are known to be worth hearing. A
course of sermons might have a 'blanket' title that would
leave each preacher free to select his own theme, for instance:

I FEEL STRONGLY THAT . . .
THE WAY FORWARD.
BEING A CHRISTIAN INVOLVES . . .
CHRISTIANITY IN THE EIGHTIES.
THE CHURCH I WOULD LIKE TO SEE.
WE HAVE TO MAKE UP OUR MINDS ABOUT . . .
WHAT HOLY COMMUNION MEANS TO ME.
IF I HAD ONLY ONE SERMON TO PREACH . . .

It may be found helpful to have a follow-up session in the hall or indeed in church after the service when, after a cup of coffee, the preacher is asked to answer questions arising out of his sermon. Another useful idea is to provide an opportunity for queries to be raised in church immediately after or even during the sermon and here the best way is to have sidesmen moving around with pencil and paper so that questions can be written down.

I have done both these things on several occasions. I have also distributed a duplicated questionnaire, asking for answers to be sent to me within a few days for comments the following Sunday. Here are the questions posed:

1. What did you think was the main point of the sermon?
2. Did you learn anything from it?
3. Did you find it difficult to follow?
4. What relevance did it have to your daily life?
5. What questions, if any, would you have liked to have asked after hearing the sermon?
6. Did you disagree with anything—and if so, what?
7. Was the sermon too long, too short or about right?
8. Did it keep your attention?
9. Do you think you will be led to do anything suggested by the sermon?
10. Any other comments?

At least some of the replies will be very helpful to the preacher, in addition to being a useful exercise for the hearer.

(4) *Lunch-hour Services*

City centre parishes have one golden opportunity for communicating that others lack. They can have lunch-hour services. There are churches where thousands of people pass the church door every weekday and in such places something can certainly be done. Lunch-hour services attract great crowds in the City of London and in many large centres.

In Guildford we began holding lunch-hour services on Fridays in Lent and soon between three hundred and four hundred people used to attend regularly, including quite a lot of school sixth-formers. We could do this because we were a city-centre parish, with thousands of people passing the church on weekdays. A good many of the courses of addresses listed in the previous section were used and we had all sorts of well-known people varying from diocesan bishops to MPs and famous stage personalities. All were professed Christians and all were highly articulate speakers. Any city-centre parish could do this sort of thing. The services began on the stroke of 1.05 p.m. with a hymn. The speaker would be introduced and would take over until 1.30 p.m., ending with a prayer.

An austerity lunch was laid on by our own people in the hall afterwards, with all the bread and cheese you wanted plus unlimited coffee. Something like half the congregation used to attend, including many of the sixth-formers. A charge of 15p (5p for students) was made but people usually gave more than this, often far more, when it was announced that total proceeds would be given to Christian Aid to feed the hungry. These Lent services met a very real need. It was noticeable that not only convinced Christians attended. Sometimes there were interested enquirers.

(5) *The Parish Magazine*

Another important means of communication is the parish magazine. Many parishes have excellent magazines, but it is a fact that others have changed to a weekly newsletter (very good in itself) and have dropped the magazine, often for reasons of economy. But a good magazine, with a professionally edited inset and the diocesan gazette, circulated to all members of the congregation (and postal copies to those who have moved away) can do an immense amount of good. Some actually make money. Those who publish at a loss should not mind this because it represents outreach and is a vital channel of communication.

There is a *Guide to Magazine Production for Churches* by Alan Robinson (Kirkfield Publications, Dewsbury) that gives much information about production, printing processes, the art work, getting it together, advertisers, paper and so on. Briefly, stencil duplicating is the best-known way of printing and is easiest and cheapest. It can be done by volunteers if you have a good typewriter and duplicator. Offset lithography is more complicated and skill and training are required if volunteers are going to be used to operate the printing machine. A plate has to be made. The end-product is far more attractive than stencil duplicating. It is probably best to find somebody who does this sort of thing professionally. Photocopying can be used, with modern machines making lithoplate or electronic stencils, but the process is expensive. The most expensive way of all is letterpress printing with metal type but this is probably out of the question for most parishes. Very many find stencil duplicating perfectly adequate.

The magazine must have an attractive appearance, with a bright and modern cover. A whole series of multicolour pictorial covers is easily obtained (they are widely advertised). The incumbent ought not to be editor. This really is a job for a layman. Excellent help with the contents is provided by the *Church News Service*. Every month some twenty columns of articles, news items, ideas, illustrations, humour and cartoons appear. The cost is about £10 a year from *Church News Service*, 37B New Cavendish Street, London W1M 8JR. I used this service for years and found it invaluable. No copyright is payable for items used.

Obviously no church magazine is going to sell well unless the appearance is attractive and the contents interesting. The editor is the key figure. The contents might include some teaching, a lot of comment about parish news and events, perhaps a letter section, maybe some humour, perhaps a competition, and certainly a letter from the incumbent. The letter need not be the first item nor need it be too long. Ways and means should be found of building up the circulation. Perhaps a distributor in every street is best, especially if the decision is made to try to appeal to a wider audience than members of the congregation. Sometimes a free circulation to every house in the parish might be considered.

Insets are important and can be obtained from commercial firms. The best known are:

The Sign, published by A. R. Mowbray and Co. Ltd, Saint Thomas House, Becket Street, Oxford OX1 1SJ. (Circulation c. 300,000 copies per month);

News Extra, published by A. R. Mowbray and Co. Ltd (Circulation c. 27,000);

Home Words, published by The Home Words Publishing Co. Ltd, PO Box 44, Guildford, Surrey GU1 1XL. (Circulation c. 175,000);

Church News, published by The Home Words Publishing Co. Ltd. (Circulation c. 120,000).

These insets are highly professional and excellent value. The usual sizes are A5 and A4, or the old crown quarto, and Mowbray and Home Words both produce splendid full colour monthly picture covers. So do The Bible Lands Society, PO Box 50, High Wycombe, Bucks. HP15 7QU. All are in colour, a different cover for each month.

A well-written, well-edited and well-produced parish magazine that includes an inset and the diocesan gazette is surely an admirable channel for communication. Readers have their attention drawn not only to parish affairs but also to diocesan ones and concerns of the wider Church. It is definitely a retrograde step when the PCC opts for packing it up in favour of a weekly newsletter. Both are wanted if the parish is to avoid becoming narrowly inward-looking.

People should also be encouraged to take a Church newspaper. The *Church Times* has the largest circulation. The *Church of England Newspaper* is also good. People have a nasty habit of borrowing somebody else's copy of a Church newspaper, thus reducing the paper's circulation. Publishing newspapers, even Church newspapers, is now such a knife-edge operation because of rising costs that it is essential for those who want to see them keep going to buy their own copies and thus increase the number of copies sold each week. Editors of both papers will send free copies to anybody undertaking a parish circulation drive.

(6) *The Weekly Newsletter*

In addition to a monthly magazine, consideration might be given to having a weekly newsletter. This is, of course, a simple matter if you are fortunate enough to have a parish secretary who is competent with a duplicator. With a newsletter there is no need to give out notices during services, where they often sound banal and monumentally unimportant. A newsletter can make them far more interesting. Attention can be drawn to matters outside the parish. There is room for comment on local affairs. Names of those on duty can be listed (people derive much simple pleasure from seeing their names in print) and Bible reading passages can be included. Do not be in the least upset if the circulation of the newsletter catches up and passes that of the monthly magazine. The monthly magazine will contain the more solid matter while the newsletter probably has the more gossipy items. It can be dictated on Friday mornings so as to be thoroughly up to date. (Mowbray produce Sunday Notice Sheets which print the collect, list the appointed psalms and readings and feature a short reflection on the gospel for the day. There is space on the other side for parish notices to be duplicated.)

(7) *The Bookstall*

A parish bookstall can be a useful aid to the spiritual life of many in the parish and any local bookshop may be asked to co-operate by supplying books on sale or return. Church bookstalls cannot buy books wholesale in order to obtain the profits for church funds but there is one useful loophole. Any organization (including any church) can apply to the Publishers Association, 19 Bedford Square, London WC1, to be registered as a book agency. You can then order books through the bookshop nominated in the application at a discount (usually ten per cent). The books must be intended for resale to the public so the scheme is not meant to provide a useful reduction in the price of hymn books or Sunday school lesson books; nor does the discount operate when books are bought on sale-or-return terms.

It is unlikely that the bookstall will pay its way. Profit-making is entirely secondary and the idea is to have well-informed Christians. The danger in having a well-stocked but unmanned bookstall in an open church is that people take the books and forget to pay, at least that is the charitable explanation of what happens all too often. The alternative is to have a person in charge and only to open the bookstall before or after service.

Of course the incumbent may choose the books he wishes his people to buy. It is good practice to feature, say, one title a month and to make frequent reference in sermon and magazine to that one book. Reasonably priced paperbacks will sell best.

I used to find that the ideal place to set up the bookstall was in the hall after the Sunday Parish Communion. People could look at it during the coffee session. There is no need to bring over everything—just a selection of books for all ages. Another good idea is to set up a small bookstall at house meetings.

A useful little book is *Managing the Church Bookstall* by the Religious Book Foundation (Hodder and Stoughton, 1980) and in it you will find all you need to know. It makes the point that about 1200 new religious books are published yearly in the UK and careful selection is needed. Different versions of the Bible at all prices should always be stocked. Christmas and anniversary cards are a good line and a second-hand book bin might be considered. Everything depends upon finding somebody keen and capable to run it but the enthusiastic support of the parish priest is essential. He can make or break it.

(8) *The Parish Library*

It is possible to set up a parish library. Cathedrals often have such libraries and very good they are, so good that setting up a separate one is not always a good idea. Usually anybody can join the cathedral library on payment of a modest subscription. Those who think a parish library would meet a need might like to know about the Bray Libraries. For a subscription of £25 you can buy £50 worth of books of your choice, renewable every two years. SPCK contribute £10,000 a year to the Bray Libraries (there are five different types) and details can be obtained from Bray Libraries, SPCK, Holy Trinity Church, Marylebone Road, London NW1 4DU.

(9) *Neighbourhood Groups*

Only a small minority come to church to hear sermons; only a minority will read the magazine or buy a book from the bookstall. But people will turn out for an evening that sounds interesting, profitable or enjoyable.

People prefer going to other people's houses rather than to church hall functions and so the neighbourhood group has developed. Groups can be set up easily enough in any sort of area but they must have a purpose, and an excellent aim is to further communication. The incumbent can either lead the groups himself or, far better, train suitable laymen. It is wise to ask for whatever conclusions may be reached to be written down and given to you, otherwise the groups may never seem to be getting anywhere and this is frustrating for all concerned.

Groups can meet every week in Lent or at any other specified time but they should then meet only occasionally, say once a month, or they will lose momentum. Another danger is that the people of a neighbourhood get to know each other well but not the people of other neighbourhoods. It is therefore sound practice to let neighbourhood groups become established and then to divide the people up into house groups all over the parish.

The groups need not be confined to known Christians; certainly in these ecumenical days the attendance should not be limited to Anglicans. The programme might often be based on Bible study or study of the current talking points; or a book might form the basis of the programme, with everybody reading a chapter a week and the group dispersing when the last chapter has been discussed.

There are a couple of books that might help those planning groups. *Open the Doors* by Edward Patey (Mowbray) stresses the need for house groups in the author's own inimitable style, while *Grow Through Groups* by Eddie Gibbs (Grove Books) stresses the underlying objects, which are to deepen commitment, to reach out into neighbouring concerns and to make disciples. The author also points out the dangers of boredom and falling numbers and has some helpful things to say about introversion, discontent and stagnation.

(10) *The Parish Conference*

Occasionally parishioners should meet not in groups but as a family and a parish conference can be very helpful. The conference can be held either at the diocesan retreat house or in the church hall; it can be arranged over a weekend, starting on a Friday evening and ending perhaps at lunchtime on Sunday. A committee of the PCC should draw up a list of subjects of parish or of general church interest to discuss and matters needing policy decisions. Goodness knows there are enough of them at the present time.

There is a lot to be said for a parish conference at the outset of a new incumbency. Careful records should be kept of all findings and conclusions and references should frequently be made to them. It is not a good thing to have perhaps a thoroughly good, stimulating and well-attended parish conference that produces all sorts of first-rate ideas, and then for nobody to hear a word about any of them ever again.

(11) *The Parish Retreat*

The parish can be called to make an extra effort for anything that is really worthwhile and in this connection thought might be given to having an annual parish retreat. Deepening the spiritual lives and general commitment of those attending is the primary object and it involves communication with God and with each other at the very deepest level. Firstly a good conductor must be found, then a booking must be made; then people should be asked to register. More people are going on retreat now than ever before and a parish that never has one may become the exception before very long. A list of retreat houses will be found in The Church of England Year Book. The Association for Promoting Retreats helps the work of the retreat houses. It publishes with the Roman Catholic Retreat Movement the magazine *The Vision* (which lists the various retreats available). The Association has a representative in every diocese.

(12) *The Press*

Good relations with the local press are important since it represents life outside the church in its most readily identifiable form. The local newspaper has considerable influence in the community and its editor is a very important man. Whether he is a Christian or not is not material, although it helps a lot if he is. His job is to see that local news, including news about the Church, is reported. The fact is that Church items interest the readers, even stories like: 'St Agatha's Mothers' Union ran a jumble sale last Saturday for branch funds. It realized the sum of £17.21 and the Vicar warmly thanked the team of helpers who made this splendid result possible.'

The editor would no doubt like to see that newsworthy parish events are covered perhaps by both a reporter and a photographer, but he is probably short-staffed and he cannot cover everything. Thus he will welcome news items which are sent in. One way is to ensure that this is done is to persuade the PCC to appoint a press officer. He can always ring the paper and give advance information or a story to the news editor; or he can write out a short report and send it in. It should be succinct and readable and if possible it should mention people's names, taking care to include the initials, ages, occupations and addresses where possible.

If the vicar has a flair for writing he might go further. He might send in a weekly sermonette or an article on some topical issue. If it is worth printing it will almost certainly be accepted, for the vicar is a man of standing in the local community and his views are of considerable interest to many. It is also important to make friends with reporters and photographers, to encourage them and to help them in every way possible to do their job well. Bear in mind that 'cub' reporters starting a career in journalism are often 'sent round the churches' as one of their first assignments. They may sometimes be awkward, but if they are treated in an off-hand manner and made to feel that they are thoroughly unwelcome intruders, then it will not help to build the good relations between Church and press that can be so valuable.

(13) *Broadcasting*

Up to a million people listen to the Sunday morning service

on Radio 4 and some television programmes reach many more than this. A broadcast is a wonderful experience for a parish church and for an incumbent. One never ceases to marvel at the enormous trouble taken by both the sound and television engineers.

There is, of course, a broadcasting technique which most of us, sadly, do not possess. You should speak fairly quickly and very clearly as you have to hold the attention of a lot of people who are probably being distracted by things going on around them. Somehow you have to give the impression that you are talking to one particular person. On the occasions when I have broadcast, I have thought particularly of those who could not come to church, patients ill in hospital, the chronic sick and the housebound, and those who are physically prevented from attending. After a broadcast letters generally rain in, indicating that the listeners are often receptive and most appreciative. Courses for the clergy are organized by the Churches Television Centre.

If you would like a broadcast to be made from your church, you should write direct to the Director of Religious Broadcasting, British Broadcasting Corporation, Broadcasting House, London W1A 1AA. The Independent Broadcasting Authority televises religious services every Sunday morning on the independent channels and in this connection one can write to the Religious Programmes Officer, Independent Broadcasting Authority, 70 Brompton Road, London SW3.

The possibilities posed by local radio are in many ways much greater. There is much more 'air-time' available. Most local radio stations have a religious programmes adviser and they will generally welcome programme suggestions and news items as well as opportunities to broadcast services from your church. These possibilities will be extended even more by the development of independent (commercial) stations.

Chapter 9

Children and Young People

(1) *Families' Services*

In some areas Families' Services are highly successful in attracting children of primary and middle-school age: five to twelve or thereabouts. This tends to be a middle-class sort of service; parents regard it as a duty to bring their children to Sunday worship even if they are not enthusiastic themselves. A new incumbent who found a flourishing Families' Service would be ill-advised to stop it; but much thought needs to be put into it. The service should last no more than forty minutes and include singing, movement and audience participation; children should read the lessons, lead the prayers and be encouraged to ask questions; they can take part in processions around the church and act as cross-bearers and acolytes; they can also elect churchwardens and sidesmen. But it requires considerable specialized knowledge (which can be acquired) and a definite talent (which cannot) if the attention of the children is to be held.

A useful booklet I can recommend for those who want detailed information about such services is *Family Services* by Kenneth Stevenson (Alcuin Club/SPCK, 1981). As there is no order for Families' Services in the ASB one concludes that the Liturgical Commission were not conscious of any particular need, but surely there is. This booklet makes out the best case I have ever seen for holding them. The author stresses the need to involve as many people as possible, and ways are suggested of including dialogue, drama, miming, dance presentations and readings from secular writers. The sample outlines suggested are imaginative and exciting.

Ideas for children's addresses can be found in many publications but perhaps *The Children's Great Texts of the Bible:* Hastings, is still the best: each sermon is an exposition of a well-known text in language children can understand, so these six volumes are by no means dated.

(2) *Sunday Schools*

Families' Services bring in the children along with their parents. A separate Sunday school brings along children whose parents do not come and who may only be interested in 'getting the kids out of the way' for at least an hour or more on a Sunday. Sunday schools tend to be linked with Sunday morning worship and the emphasis is on leading the children on to adult worship. The weakness of the Families' Service is that when the children are over the age of eleven, they feel they are too old to attend; but when it is suggested that they graduate to full-scale Mattins they find a congregation of elderly people and a service which to them is dull and boring.

It often works well to bring the children to the start of Mattins, have a special talk for children after the second lesson and then let them leave for Sunday school, coming back to meet their parents after the service is over.

It is more satisfactory to integrate Sunday school with worship in parishes which have a Parish Communion. Whole families can be encouraged to come, no matter what age the children are, which is why a crèche is vital. Young children attend only a part of the service because the last thing we want is to bore them. The major question is: should the children come in for the first part of the service, leaving church immediately after the gospel; or should they go direct to Sunday school and all come in for what used to be called the Consecration prayer but is now called the Thanksgiving? if the children leave after the gospel their parents can enter fully into the most solemn part of the service and neither they nor other members of the congregation are disturbed by the antics of the young children and maybe the restlessness of slightly older ones. On the other hand, the teachers can make their communions with the rest of the parish where the children come in for the *missa fidelium*. The children can come up to the altar to receive a blessing. Both children and teachers feel they really belong and from the earliest years the children become familiar with the sacred mysteries.

There is something to be said for both. Where the children leave after the gospel, making concentration possible for mother and father (and others) during the most solemn part, we are moving in line with the Church in its earliest days. There the idea was to exclude the unconfirmed and the uninstructed from the central part of the Eucharist, thus avoiding any possible cheapening. Psychologically this is sound practice for children. They love having something 'grown-up' to which they can look forward. But, on the whole, I think it best to adopt the second method. Let Sunday school begin at once. Let the children come in during the offertory hymn. Let them come up to the altar to receive a blessing. This method ensures that whole families are together at the crucial point. It also ensures that teachers can make their communions and not to have to come to the 8 a.m. celebration. As the children are only in church for a short while disturbance is unlikely to be very great.

What sort of course should be followed in Sunday school? Here the diocesan education officer or Sunday school adviser should be consulted. There are many first-class teaching courses with visual aids and practical work available and these should be bought and used. The Church of England Board of Education through the Church Information Office and the National Society for Promoting Religious Education through SPCK publish numerous courses of a very high standard. Books and materials are available from religious bookshops. *Teaching Christianity* by Mabel Hayes (Mowbray 1982/1983) will be found useful by those who want resource books and lesson books with worksheets. Money spent on teaching aids for Sunday schools ought to be one of the top priorities in a live parish: it is a short-sighted PCC which does not invest in education.

The crèche will look after infants up to the age of three. The junior Sunday school will cover what is likely to be the biggest age group: the three to eight year olds. The senior school will take the eight to eleven group. After eleven it is likely that the children will feel that they have outgrown Sunday school and they should be encouraged to attend the whole Parish Communion service, sitting with their parents rather than with each other. When they come to Confirmation classes a year later they will already know a great deal about the Holy Communion service.

Children should be encouraged to come into the hall for the coffee or tea sessions, the *agape*, immediately after service. For them lemonade and biscuits should be provided free of charge and, if there is another room or hall available, they will enjoy having the run of the youth club games. They will not want to stay with their parents, wondering when their parents will tire of talking and move off home.

(3) *Confirmation Preparation*

The method of Confirmation preparation is vital. The classes should begin at about the same time each year and people should be invited to register if they are interested. There should be one class for those under fifteen and one for those over. The classes should continue for six months, with a fortnight's break in between. The object must be to do far more than just communicate information; it is nothing less than to lead to informed Christian commitment, to acceptance of Jesus as Lord. We need to encourage discussion and once the ice has been broken this is not usually difficult, provided the groups are not too large or too small. Perhaps about a dozen is the ideal size, so that all sorts of viewpoints can be put forward while everybody can have a chance to contribute. The course should be firmly based on the Creed, the Ten Commandments, the Lord's Prayer and the remainder of the Revised Catechism. Everything essential can be touched on and film strips are available to help. Near the end, one class, I believe, should be lead by three laymen, one talking for a few minutes on 'How we run our church', another 'What my confirmation meant to me', the third 'What Holy Communion means to me'. The first communion is generally made on the Sunday following confirmation and much should be made of this, welcoming the newly confirmed publicly at the beginning of Family Communion.

Some experienced parish priests believe it right to admit candidates to communion before confirmation, particularly when there is some indication that they are 'ready and desirous of being confirmed'. Some believe we should admit children as young as eight or nine to receive the sacrament, thus following Roman Catholic practice, and there are several dioceses where, with the permission of the bishop, this is being tried. Some of us are as yet unpersuaded that this is likely to be a good thing because we are of the opinion that to take away the eager looking forward to something is unlikely to be helpful.

I can recommend some helpful books. *Towards Confirmation* by John Eddison (Marshall, Morgan and Scott, 1982) might interest some of the brighter candidates. *Confirmation Cook Book* by David Manship (Mowbray, 1980) was drawn up by the Winchester diocesan education team and contains a new and surprising system of confirmation preparation, far less formal than anything else I have ever seen. It is good.

Follow-up is important. *A Pocket Guide to the Anglican Church* (a revised edition of the earlier *After Confirmation*) by

R. H. Lloyd (Mowbray, 1984) is by the Precentor of Christ Church Cathedral, Oxford, and former chaplain of the Dragon School at Oxford, and discusses important aspects of Christian belief. Confirmation classes naturally end with the actual service but there is much to be said for continuing to meet at intervals, with the emphasis on discussion rather than monologue. It is still helpful to present to each candidate a suitable manual, one which should be given to them well beforehand. They should be taken carefully through it and encouraged to use it regularly. There is a good *Communicant's Manual* by William Purcell (Mowbray, 1981, 1984) with editions based on both Rite A and Rite B of the ASB. There is also the much fuller *In His Presence* by Denis E. Taylor (Religious Education Press, 1982), a re-issue again based on Rite A/Rite B of the ASB. *Draw Near with Faith—a Confirmation Prayer Book* by Geoffrey Shilvock (Mowbray, 1984) will also be found useful.

Some parish priests urge their candidates to make their confessions beforehand and this certainly makes sense. But I prefer to see every candidate privately, shortly before the actual confirmation, and to ask these three questions—Why do you want to be confirmed? Was there anything in the classes you did not really understand? What do you reckon is your chief fault? This private interview is rather dreaded by some perhaps but soon a relaxed atmosphere is established and the whole thing is helpful. Some take their candidates away for a weekend retreat at the diocesan retreat house and this can do nothing but good.

(4) *Closed Youth Clubs*

It is essential that there should be lively, interesting Parish Communion where the young people will not feel too conspicuous. Young people like to see a lot of other young people around, like to feel that they belong to something that others consider worthwhile. This is where a closed youth club is valuable. Open clubs are easier to run of course and many of them are most successful in terms of numbers, though the local authority generally runs them even better. The closed youth club exists for a different purpose: it has definite rules and the young people themselves usually see their point. No one resents the rule about attending Parish Communion, for they would be unlikely to join in the first place if they did. Members can bring guests who have nothing to do with the church and it is heartening to see some of these guests come to church and find, to their great surprise perhaps, that Parish Communion means something to them. I know many who have been led to full Christian commitment by this method. The club members should meet often for discussion in private houses, for young people very much enjoy each other's company, love talking and find it easier to do this in a private house in groups that are not over-large. Where it is possible for the youth group or groups to meet three times a week, some local authorities are prepared to make a grant to pay the leader.

(5) *Church Day Schools*

Religious education is the only subject all schools are compelled to teach under the 1944 Education Act (which is still in force); also, every school has to hold morning assembly. Religious teaching in local authority schools is non-denominational and often indifferent, unenthusiastic and felt to be a waste of time. However, of nearly 8 million children in maintained schools in England in 1983 no less than 10.9 per cent (840,311 children) were at Church of England schools. There are three types. There were 3,143 Controlled schools, 2,166 Aided schools and 20 Special Agreement schools.

In Aided schools the links with the parish church are clear and definite. The PCC and church organizations appoint a majority of the governors and the incumbent is usually chairman. The governing body appoints the teachers and thus they may select a teaching staff consisting wholly of communicant Anglicans. There is a 'right of entry' for clergy to go in to give denominational religious teaching and for the whole school to attend services in church. The Church has to find an annual contribution that enables the governors to meet fifteen per cent of the cost of structural repairs and of rebuilding. By the terms of the 1980 Education Act the term 'managers' was dropped and 'governors' substituted.

Controlled schools are still church schools but the Church appoints only a minority of governors and these governors do not have the right to appoint teachers. The Church does not have to make a contribution but the parish church still has certain rights about using the school buildings and the clergy have certain rights of entry. Generally speaking, denominational teaching can be given if the parents want it. If the clergy wish to enter the school a great deal for teaching purposes, it must be with the goodwill of the head teacher. In many Controlled schools the clergy come and go as often as they do in Aided schools. The governing body has a voice in Controlled schools, in the appointment of one reserved teacher who is qualified to teach religious education.

Many parents greatly value the part played by a church school and often opt for one rather than a local authority school. If they are churchgoers, they may think the church emphasis important. If they are not, they may suppose the school will make up for their own deficiencies in teaching religion to their children. Perhaps, most important of all, there is a feeling that a church school is more likely to produce the kind of child the parents want to see. Full information about the advantages of a Church of England Aided School can be obtained from the Board of Education, Church House, Dean's Yard, London SW1P 3NZ or from the National Society for Promoting Religious Education (at the same address). The National Society also helps with small grants towards the building and extension of Church schools and provides a legal and advisory service.

Some Church of England Aided school buildings are hopelessly out of date and often require complete rebuilding on a new site. But in many areas neither the diocese nor the parish has available the vast sum required for rebuilding, no less than fifteen per cent of the total cost. One possible solution is to apply for Controlled instead of the existing Aided status. The diocesan director of religious education will advise and so will the local authority education officer. I did this in Guildford, thus sparing the parish the commitment of raising some £40,000. I found my church had lost almost nothing and I continued to go into the school and teach exactly as before. But it is true (though surely very unlikely) that the head might be a non-Christian or lacking in goodwill. In that event I can see that any effective church contact might be lost. Where the diocese or parish can find the money to rebuild or modernize it is probably better not to apply for Controlled status. When an Aided school is closed, the site can be sold and the money would normally be made available to help other Aided schools in the diocese. By the way, the Board of Education is currently trying to get the law changed so that schools may transfer from Controlled to Aided status. Curiously, the law does not at present permit this. There is one problem that must arise fairly frequently. What ought the aims of a church school to be in a multi-faith area?

(6) *Youth Organizations*

Many parishes find great value in the well-known organizations that are found in all parts of the country. The Scouts and Guides are the best known and the most popular. Some churches have open Scout and Guide companies (i.e. open to anybody who is prepared to observe the rules) and some closed (i.e. confined to church members only). The right procedure for starting a group is to get in touch with the district commissioner or to write to headquarters. The Scout Association's address is Baden-Powell House, Queen's Gate, London SW7 5JS and the Girl Guide Association's is 17/19 Buckingham Palace Road, London SW1W 0PT. It is worth noting that in 1983 there were 641,000 scouts in this country, of which one-third were in groups sponsored by Anglican churches.

The Church Lads' Brigade and the Church Girls' Brigade amalgamated in 1978 to form this exclusively Anglican organization. All officers have to be communicant members of the Church. I can testify that this uniformed organization is very good. The address of headquarters is Claude Hardy House, 15 Etchingham Park Road, Finchley, London N3 2DU. I also had a branch of the Girls' Friendly Society and Townsend Fellowship and found it excellent. Again, it is based on the parochial unit. Activities include adventure holidays, leadership training and provision of hostels and holiday houses. Headquarters address—126 Queen's Gate, London SW7 5LQ. There are several other national youth organizations that have done and are doing valuable work in bringing out the best in our young people. They seem to appeal to a particular type and hold their loyalty and interest to a greater extent than do ordinary youth clubs.

Some think there has been a move away from uniformed organizations. I don't believe it. I suspect there are more Scouts and Guides, for instance, than ever. The real difficulties are finding suitable leaders and suitable meeting-places. The local church is well situated to find both. Many of us would love to see the old organizations re-establishing themselves in parish after parish where at present young people are conspicuously absent. Probably open groups are to be preferred to closed ones (it would be almost impossible to get the latter off the ground in many places) but a reasonable minimum of one church parade per month would not be difficult.

Chapter 10

The Occasional Offices

(1) *Holy Baptism*

Much time is taken up with matters connected with the occasional offices: Holy Baptism, the Solemnization of Matrimony and the Burial of the Dead. The first two create opportunities for contact with people perhaps leading to full Christian commitment.

The majority of parents want their babies baptized. To quote a random figure, the average for the whole country in 1981 was 365 Church of England baptisms per 1,000 live births. When you add the Roman Catholic and Nonconformist figures and the number of those turned away by clergy of rigorist outlook it must indeed be true that a majority of parents really do want this sacrament, whether they understand it or not. I happen to be chaplain of the local maternity hospital and I have asked dozens of mothers whether they want this. The answer is nearly always yes. It is still considered the right thing to do. In some cases the parents want a big family get-together, in others it is social convention, maybe in a few cases it is pure superstition. I feel there is something here upon which we can build. It is not really helpful to say firmly that we will not baptize the babies of any except regular churchgoers.

Canon B21 encourages the minister to 'administer the sacrament of Holy Baptism on Sundays at public worship when the most number of people come together, that the congregation there present may witness the receiving of them that be newly baptized into Christ's Church, and be put in remembrance of their own profession made to God in their baptism'. If the minister refuses to baptize for any reason, Canon B22.2 states: 'the parents or guardians may apply to the bishop of the diocese, who shall, after consultation with the minister, give such directions as he thinks fit'. Not many aggrieved parents know this. If they did, the diocesan bishop might get a rain of requests and in most cases he would probably ask a neighbouring incumbent to perform this duty. Canon B22.3 states that the minister shall instruct the parents while Canon B22.4 firmly adds: 'No minister shall refuse or, save for the purpose of preparing or instructing the parents or guardians, delay to baptize any infant within his cure . . .'. This makes clear the official view of the Church of England; clearly rigorism is not encouraged. Some of us feel that when parents come to us for the baptism of their child we are given a priceless pastoral opportunity. Full use should be made of it.

When the parents come to ask for baptism a date and time should be fixed and the necessary form filled in (SPCK publish an excellent one). A letter or a leaflet should be given to the parents explaining baptism (Mowbray publish a splendid Baptism Information Sheet, containing very clear items of information for parents and godparents. It deserves to be widely used). A date should be fixed for instruction in the parents' home; the godparents may also be invited to attend. The instruction should explain what baptism is and, of course, stress the Christian commitment assumed in those who make the promises. We should make the most of a great opportunity, for time and again parents can be brought to confirmation classes. The baptism service itself is a great occasion for all; the one in the ASB is deservedly popular. Ideally baptism should be administered at public worship with lighted candles and congregational participation. At Parish Communion it should follow the Gospel; at Morning or Evening Prayer it follows the second lesson. Where baptisms are very numerous consideration might be given to having them on a Sunday afternoon, monthly or quarterly or, best of all, at the great festivals, with perhaps ten babies or so at a time, with the full choir attending, with bells ringing, and with the PCC and members of the congregation encouraged to attend. In such a case all concerned should come to a rehearsal the previous Sunday afternoon. The PCC and members of the congregation living in the same street might also come to meet the parents, welcome them and perhaps volunteer to act as additional church godparents. A cup of tea and social gathering after the rehearsal is worthwhile.

Obviously it is highly desirable that baptisms should take place at the main Sunday service in accordance with the Canon (which might have added something to the effect that the idea is so that the congregation can also warmly welcome its newest members). But what of a parish with a very large number of baptisms? I served my title in a parish where there were often twenty in a single week. Obviously baptisms held nearly every Sunday would become a nuisance and any incumbent must surely take note of the word 'normally' in the Canon. I can testify that the afternoon arrangement I have mentioned often filled the church and frequently greatly impressed those taking part. The trend today is emphatically to discourage virtually private baptisms in the presence only of friends and relatives of one baby only. This survival of Georgian snobbery is surely on the way out.

Where you are asked to baptize a baby from another parish, care should be taken. Many requests will come from disgruntled parents who have been turned down by their own parish priest. You may agree to accept those with even slight claims upon you. The parents may have been married in your church; perhaps they used to live in the parish; perhaps their parents had strong connections. If none of these conditions apply, the parents should be told that they should attend church for at least six months and so establish the right to be entered on the electoral roll. Otherwise their parish priest may be asked to signify his approval by signing the baptism form 'no objection'. If he refuses to do this he does not have the power of veto, for Canon B22(5) states: 'A minister who intends to baptize any infant whose parents are residing outside the boundaries of his cure, unless the names of such persons or of one of them be on the church electoral roll of the same, shall not proceed to the baptism without having sought the goodwill of the minister of the parish in which such parents reside.'

No fee is payable in connection with a baptism except for a baptism certificate. A baptism register must be kept. Follow-up is very important; cards can be sent on the baptism anniversaries and every encouragement given to the child to attend first the crèche and then the Sunday school. It is unlikely to do either unless the parents are willing to become involved.

(2) *The Godparents*

Canon B23 lays down the requirements about godparents. Godparents play an important part in Anglican baptism formularies and have done ever since the 1549 Prayer Book. The Canon states that there must be at least three, of whom at least two shall be of the same sex as the child and one of the opposite sex. If necessity requires it then one godmother and one godfather will suffice. Parents can be godparents provided there is at least one other.

Godparents should themselves be baptized and confirmed but the minister 'shall have power to dispense with the requirement of confirmation in any case in which in his judgement need so requires'. Some take the choice of godparents very seriously, in other cases it is clearly a farce. Godparents should not be chosen just to please somebody— an elderly grandmother for instance—nor should possible later financial advantage be a qualification. It should be regarded as an honour to be asked to be a godparent. The least the godparents should be expected to do is to pray regularly for the child, set a good example, take a keen interest in him/her and generally be regarded as a friend. There is no reason why the godparent should not be a keen practising Free Church member or Roman Catholic, provided they can make the necessary undertakings and say all the appropriate words with a good conscience.

(3) *A Service of Thanksgiving*

The recommendation that a new service of Thanksgiving should be prepared was carefully examined by the Archbishops' Commission on Christian Doctrine in the Report, *Baptism, Thanksgiving and Blessing* (Ramsey Commission, GS 56, 1971) which warmly endorsed the suggestion that a service of Thanksgiving should be offered to parents who wish to defer baptism or who are not regular churchgoers. There must be no suggestion of reception into the Church and no godparents; nor should the giving of the name be part of the service. The service might conveniently take place in the home and must not be associated with the font. There should be no official register of children for whose birth thanks to God have been offered. It should not be regarded as a substitute for baptism; indeed the hope is that in due course the child will be brought for baptism.

These suggestions have been adopted by the Liturgical Commission and in the ASB, under the heading Initiation Services, there are services of Thanksgiving for the Birth of a Child and Thanksgiving after Adoption. But neither of these services is intended to be a special naming of the child and a substitute for baptism. Rather are they intended to take the place of the old Thanksgiving of Women after Child-birth. That old service certainly had superstitious overtones in East London years ago and seemed to suggest ritual impurity on the old Jewish scale. We can of course still use it if asked but the new ones are far better. Ideally the new services should be used at the Eucharist, when father and mother and the whole family can give thanks. If the baptism is planned to follow immediately afterwards the need for either service is not very apparent.

(4) *Adult Baptism*

The service of adult baptism is likely to be required more frequently in the future than in the past. If a great many babies are refused baptism by their parish priest it seems reasonable to suppose that quite a number will want to be baptized when they can make up their own minds. The thought in the ASB is that 'Our circumstances today point to the need for a single service of Christian initiation which includes in a single occasion the elements of baptism, confirmation and holy communion' (*A Commentary by the Liturgical Commission*). It makes the point that 'adult baptisms tend to increase'.

Adult candidates must of course be carefully prepared. They will attend classes and it will be assumed that those who want baptism will also want confirmation. What do you do with those who, after preparation, still want baptism only? Canon B24.3 is clear that 'Every person thus baptized shall be confirmed by the bishop as soon after his baptism as conveniently may be: that so he may be admitted to the Holy Communion'.

Some hold that adult baptism ought to be the norm, the belief held by the Baptist Church. Baptists believe that only believer's baptism is genuine. There is nothing in our formularies that indicates a move away from infant baptism. Those who have any hesitations might like to look at *Children of Promise* by Geoffrey Bromley (T. and T. Clark, 1979). It sets out the historical arguments very clearly. There is also *Christian Baptism* by Philip Crowe (Mowbray, 1980) which is a very clear and easy-to-read statement and ideal to give to parents.

(5) *Christian Marriage: The Law*

There are those who hold that marriage is on the way out as

more and more couples set up house together and dispense with what they derisively call 'a piece of paper'. I am one of those who see this as a passing phase, a reaction against parental and other authority; it will surely pass just as soon as girls see that they are throwing away the security that it has taken centuries to build up for them and for their children. Merely living together is a very poor substitute for the genuine thing even though it seems to be socially acceptable in this permissive age. The fact remains that marriage, particularly marriage in church, is still seen to be the ideal, the thing that most responsible people want. What a wonderful opportunity this gives us.

Firstly, we should know something of the law of the land. No person under the age of sixteen can be married; in the case of persons under eighteen, it is highly desirable to raise difficulties, for it is surely often far too young. It is permitted to read the banns of minors and thus leave it to the parents to forbid the banns on grounds of age but I always find it far better to go and see the parents myself and see if written consent is likely to be given. Any parishioner over the age of sixteen has the right to marriage in the parish church or in the church on the electoral roll of which his name is entered but we are under no obligation to make easy such marriages, which are often lightly entered into.

Marriages can be after banns or by licence. Banns and licences are valid for three months. Marriages can only be celebrated between the hours of 8 a.m. and 6 p.m. After the marriage the officiating clergyman must see that the details are entered into duplicate registers provided by the Registrar General and copies of the entries must be sent to the local registrar quarterly. If you are marrying somebody whose name is on your electoral roll, then banns must be published in the parishes where each party resides and in yours. The marriage cannot be solemnized unless written evidence is received that the banns have been properly called and no impediment alleged. The banns must be called on three Sundays, but they need not be successive ones. Most marriages are after banns, but they can be solemnized on the authority of a common licence or special licence or on the authority of a certificate issued by a superintendent registrar. Such certificates are rarely seen. Marriages by special licence are also rare. This licence, granted by the Archbishop of Canterbury, permits marriage in any place at any time (in, say, a hospital). Common licences are granted by the bishop of the diocese and people who want one—people who want to get married in a hurry for instance—usually apply to what is called a surrogate (there is one incumbent in each area who is so appointed) who in turn forwards the application to the diocesan registrar. The licence may cost about £21 and can usually be obtained by return of post.

Before arranging to have banns published or a licence obtained, persons must know in which parish they reside. It may come as a surprise to incumbents to discover that a very large number of their parishioners do not have the faintest idea which parish they live in. Applicants should be advised to ring up the incumbent they think most likely to be their parish priest. He will almost certainly have in his possession a map marking the parish boundaries and, if the incumbent has no such map, the applicant should certainly get in touch with the diocesan office to find out where precisely the boundaries are.

The position is more complicated when one of those getting married is a foreign national. In that event, a common licence is needed and the couple concerned should apply themselves to the diocesan registrar. He requires written evidence that the marriage will be recognized as valid in the foreign country concerned. Incumbents do well to obtain *Suggestions for the Guidance of the Clergy* issued by the Registrar General in 1982. It includes detailed instructions for entering full particulars in the registers.

(6) *Christian Marriage: Preparation*

The couple coming to the vicarage want far more than

information; they want help and guidance. Having established that the people have a right to be married in your church they should be given two 'Application for the Publication of Banns' forms (a piece of carbon paper can be put between them to save needless labour). One form is for you and the other for the parish clerk; it contains everything that has to be entered into the marriage register. The couple can be left alone for ten minutes to do this. Then with the application in front of you, you can ask questions about Christian allegiance: why they want a marriage in church; how far they accept the Christian doctrine of marriage. This interview constitutes the greatest evangelistic opportunity the parish priest ever has. I have signed on dozens of confirmation candidates through this means just because I believe that if a couple are willing to accept Christian commitment their hopes of a truly happy marriage are vastly increased. They must also be told about practical things and it is as well to have a duplicated sheet for them to take away: who to see about the music and when; who to see about the flowers; the cost of the marriage and of all the extras together with any local details you think necessary.

At this interview it is right to ask the couple which form of service they want, 1662, Series 2 or ASB. The young people may have no idea that there are two services and that the choice is theirs. A quick run-through will soon make clear the difference. It would also be helpful to discover whether the bride wishes to include 'obey' or not. They should be given time to go away and talk things over.

A second interview a month or so before the wedding is necessary. You can then check banns publications, choice of service and precisely what the couple really want (including the music, if any). Then you can go through the service with them clause by clause. Most couples will be grateful if you talk to them about personal relationships, about money and the need for a carefully-worked out budget, about housing and mortgages and insurance policies, about the sexual side and about the spiritual side. This is certainly rather a lot to pack into an hour or so and it may be that the local marriage guidance council either runs courses for engaged couples or would be willing to do so. A lot of couples know a great deal about the sexual side and certainly do not want to discuss it. But I have found that most do, particularly if it includes a clear statement of the Christian position.

The couple will almost certainly welcome a rehearsal of the ceremony in church. This can be held at any convenient time, when the couple and people like the bride's father, the best man and the bridesmaids can come. You go through the whole service from start to finish, explaining exactly what is said, where everybody stands and so on. A good way of ending the rehearsal is to say a prayer.

At the actual service I always like to have a word with the bridegroom beforehand (he is usually extremely nervous!). I always prefer the bridegroom to come into the vestry with the best man before the service to check the registers and settle the fees, thus avoiding the need to produce money afterwards. I meet the bride at the door (she is often very nervous too!). I welcome the congregation from the chancel step and tell them why they are there and what they are supposed to do. A short address from the chancel step immediately after the actual marriage ceremony is highly desirable, setting out the meaning and purpose of Christian marriage. A few words can be spoken to the couple alone at the chancel step before the final hymn. It seems to me that more and more couples who are churchgoers now want a nuptial mass and excellent provision for this is made in the ASB. There the marriage service is structured so that it can (a) be set within the Eucharist, (b) follow the traditional pattern and end with readings and prayers or (c) follow the traditional pattern and conclude with the Eucharist. It is important that the couple should decide precisely what they want but help and guidance from you will be welcomed.

(7) *A Service of Blessing*

Something like one in three of all marriages in this country ends in divorce. The General Synod has now given approval in principle to the remarriage of divorced people in church but not everybody thinks this is right and not every divorced person wants such a service anyway. It seems likely that there will always be a need for a service of blessing following a registry office marriage; I have taken part in a great many such services. It is not difficult to draw up something suitable, indeed there is probably an approved form in the diocese. It should include a statement of what the service is for, suitable readings from the Bible, the promises, the blessing of the ring, a psalm, hymns and prayers. I always give a Bible to the couple as they kneel at the chancel step, with the words: 'I give you this Bible. May the word of God be a light to your path.' The General Synod has also instructed the Liturgical Commission to prepare a service of prayer and dedication which would replace diocesan forms of service.

Such a service as this may well be used where the couple do not feel it right to have the full marriage service or where you do not feel you can recommend them to the bishop for the full service. This service of blessing has, to my certain knowledge, been much appreciated by the couple, by their families and by their friends. It is a service of joy and in it penitence plays no part. The place for penitence is not here but beforehand. I never could see any point in making it a low-key non-event. It ought to be a truly great occasion, one the couple will always remember. Admission to Holy Communion is now a matter not for the bishop but for the parish priest.

(8) *The Remarriage of Divorced People in Church*

According to the law of the land we are able to marry in church someone with a former partner still living and we can do so without reference to the bishop or to anybody else. This has not however been the common practice. The Convocation Regulations passed in 1957 stated that such services ought not to be conducted in church and the Matrimonial Causes Act of 1950 provided that we could forbid the use of our churches for such purposes. Generally speaking, the clergy were unwilling to defy the expressed mind of our Church, although there were exceptions. When devout Christians who had been through the trauma of a divorce came to us for help all we could do was to offer them a service of blessing. Some clergy insisted on even this being a travesty of anything associated with joy.

But many clergy were unhappy about it all. They knew that the Eastern Orthodox Church remarried divorced people. They knew that the Free Churches raised no particular difficulties in genuine cases, total discretion being left to the minister concerned. They knew that the Roman Catholic Church, seemingly so intransigent, allowed marriages to be annulled on many and varied grounds not open to us or any other Church. The Church of England was, without doubt, the strictest Church in Christendom.

But there have for long been clear signs of a change of thought. An Archbishops' Commission produced a Report *Marriage, Divorce and the Church* in 1971 which recommended that remarriage in church should be permitted in certain circumstances. Nobody can accuse the Church of England of breathless haste. It was not until 1983 that the General Synod at the July meeting in York passed a resolution affirming that the remarriage of divorced people in church could, subject to certain conditions, be allowed. The incumbent would first of all decide if the people concerned were genuine in their acceptance of the Christian doctrine of marriage. He would make a recommendation to the bishop, who would refer the matter to a small commission. If and when permission was given the incumbent could proceed. The bishop would dispense the divorced person from previous vows.

This decision was not greeted with general satisfaction. Some accused the Church of England of lowering the whole tone of marriage discipline and making it more difficult for couples to keep their vows. Others said that at last the Church of England had shown an awareness that ours is the religion of the second chance. For long we have accepted that people who remarry after divorce are not living in adultery. They have been admitted to communion, can be on the electoral roll and may serve as church councillors and churchwardens. At the time of writing no agreed procedure has been accepted. It is certain that remarriage in church will be accepted as possible and desirable in certain cases but certainly not for all and sundry. The trouble is that, whatever the agreed procedure, some incumbents will be far too strict and some far too lax. One can only hope that there will be no weakening of the stress laid on the desirability of perman- ance in the marriage relationship, no watering down of a high doctrine of episcopacy and no diminution of the heed paid to the clearly expressed mind of our Church. No doubt clear guidelines will in due course be agreed by General Synod.

Those who want a scholarly study of Christian marriage rites will find everything they want in *Nuptial Blessing* by Kenneth Stevenson (Alcuin Club/SPCK, 1982). *To Have and to Hold* by David Atkinson (Collins, 1979) contains a thoughtful study of the ethical and pastoral questions raised by divorce and remarriage.

(9) *The Burial of the Dead*

It is best to call on the bereaved members of the family in their home as soon as possible after hearing about a death. In former days the body was usually in the house and the minister was invited to view it. I always invited the members of the family to come with me for a prayer of commendation. This custom is now out and bodies are customarily kept in the undertaker's chapel of rest or the local mortuary until the funeral. Your help will be much appreciated in making the necessary arrangements. Is there to be a service in church? Will it be at the cemetery chapel? Will it all be at the crematorium? Will there be organ music? Will there be hymns? Are there to be printed service papers? Does the family want the old 1662 service, Series 1 or the ASB?

Great care must be taken when reading the burial service, for any suggestion of haste or lack of preparation is keenly resented. Many families very much appreciate a few words spoken at a funeral, the more so when trouble has clearly been taken. After the funeral you should take it as a compliment and not a nuisance if you are invited back to the family gathering for a meal.

Sometimes there are masses of flowers at a funeral but the custom of elaborate (and very expensive) wreaths and crosses is fast dying out. It is becoming more and more usual for a request to be made for family flowers only and a note in the newspaper saying that donations may be sent if desired to some named charity or good cause. More and more cremations are taking place. There is a lot to be said for having a Garden of Remembrance in the churchyard. Ashes ought always to be interred; the practice of scattering them is to be deplored. Some Gardens of Remembrance have small commemorative stones; in other places the custom is to have a Book of Remembrance in a special cabinet in church.

Mourners often display great courage and fortitude right up to the funeral day. It is after it is all over and friends and relatives have returned home that reaction sets in and it is then that visits from the clergy can be specially valuable.

Chapter 11

The Sick and the Frail

(1) *The Object*

The Book of Common Prayer has an Order for the Visitation of the Sick that, one imagines, few parish priests have ever used. The language and the approach are out of date and that is that. But it does make an important assumption, and that is that when we call on a sick person at home or in hospital we are going for a purpose, a purpose that has something to do with our ministry. Sick people are often very puzzled when the parson calls and discusses the weather, the news from Ulster or prospects for the Derby—and nothing else other than trivialities. When a doctor visits patients he talks about the state of their health. People are entitled to expect the parson to show some concern about the state of their souls and at least some will be disappointed if, for example, no prayers are said. The 1662 Visitation of the Sick includes prayers and readings and practical directions. Does the sick man repent of his sins? Is he in charity with everybody? Is there any wrong he ought to put right? Has he made a will? All these are practical questions which the parish priest alone has a right to ask. Take the last question. I have often helped people to draw up wills, usually ones disposing of very small

138

sums of money. Where larger sums are involved it is always best to suggest that a solicitor should be called in.

(2) *A Healing Ministry*

There is no Order for the Visitation of the Sick in the ASB but a separate one appeared in 1983 called *Ministry to the Sick*, and very good it is. It includes Communion with the Sick, the Laying on of Hands with Prayer, Anointing, a Commendation at the Time of Death, Prayers for use with the Sick and a list of suggested psalms and readings. A separate card is obtainable, containing the Distribution of Holy Communion and the Laying on of Hands and Anointing. I have used this card very many times. The Laying on of Hands and Anointing are much appreciated and somehow the fact that it is all printed on a card makes it more acceptable. The card makes it abundantly plain that we have an important role to play in the way of care, comfort and healing.

When visiting a sick person and the talk seems to be moving round to private matters, the parish priest should not hesitate to ask other people to leave the room. Visiting sometimes leads a sick person to impart highly confidential information, even to making a special confession of sin. Often relieving the patient's mind may lead to the healing of his body—and as a parish priest and hospital chaplain of long standing I could quote case after case to prove this point. Ours is certainly a healing ministry; we have good news to bring. We can talk about the patient's worries if that is what he wants. We can say a prayer for healing. We can give the laying on of hands. We can anoint with oil in the way suggested in James 5.13–15. There are some admirable suggestions in *Ministry to the Sick*.

All healing comes from God. The Church now seems to be stressing this important fact more and more and it is not unusual to have healing services in church. Sometimes this healing is incorporated in the Parish Communion, often at the end. Anybody wanting healing simply kneels at the communion rail, with friends and supporters standing around. The parish priest goes from person to person, enquiring what he is to pray for and then giving the laying on of hands. Sometimes special healing services are held, often featuring somebody with healing gifts. The former seems to me to be good but the latter rather questionable because not the sort of thing that has New Testament authority.

(3) *The Dying*

When a Roman Catholic is close to death, whether at home or in hospital, it is customary to send for the priest. It is nothing like so customary with Anglicans, one reason being that death is the great modern taboo, something never mentioned, never even hinted at and only rarely prepared for. We ought to make it known that we are ready and willing to be sent for and that we will always come, at any hour of the day or night.

Sometimes people are so gravely ill or so heavily sedated that it seems impossible to communicate with them. In such cases, simply to hold the hand of the sick person is valuable, for the human touch is of far greater consequence than is commonly realized. The simplest and best-known prayers are appreciated, always including the Lord's Prayer. Even if the sick person is deeply unconscious, indeed to all appearances dead to the world, you should know that the sense of hearing is the last to go. Time and again I have seen the 'unconscious' person's lips move and he either joins in something well-known or perhaps says amen. There are some excellent commendatory prayers in *Ministry to the Sick* but you may feel extempore prayers are best both for the sick man and for his relatives.

Ought a dying person to be told the truth or is a policy of concealing it better? I used to think a dying person ought always to be told, whether he asks or not, but I have now changed my views. Some people simply do not want to be told. They do not ask anybody anything and they show no awareness that death may be close. They have a right to their views. What cannot be defended is to lie in response to a definite request to be told everything. Many really do want to know and when this is so it is common for doctors to tell them. The clergy have a role here too. Often they are the best people to do the telling because they can at once go on to talk about preparation, about putting things right, about belief in God, about Jesus Christ and about life beyond the grave. They can read appropriate passages and say appropriate prayers. By the way, you should note that few doctors ever say: 'You are going to die. You have a matter of a few days left.' It is much more likely that they will say something like: 'Your X-ray plates show this. What we are doing is this. You have to face the fact that you may not recover. Meanwhile we are doing all we possibly can.' The doctors are careful not to be too definite because they are so often wrong. Dying people sometimes inexplicably get better. The parson must be equally circumspect. It cannot be right to take away all hope.

(4) *The Reserved Sacrament*

Sick people often like to receive Holy Communion at home and in larger parishes there ought to be a list of elderly and housebound people who receive it monthly. Some clergy celebrate with practically the whole communion service every time, using a cross, lit candles and a small private communion set. This is very much appreciated but it can be very time consuming if there are a large number of people on the list. The shortened form on the card from *Ministry to the Sick* is perfectly adequate, using the reserved sacrament. Communicants like to know that they are receiving the elements consecrated at the previous Parish Communion, where they were prayed for by name. There is another way that is being increasingly used. This is for licensed lay assistants to take the consecrated elements straight from the altar, immediately after receiving themselves, to the sick or old person. This is surely an admirable idea, soundly based on New Testament practice.

There may well be a need for the sacrament to be reserved in any parish, especially if the incumbent is a part-time hospital chaplain. The simplest way of reserving is by intinction. You break a consecrated wafer in half: dip the end into the chalice: touch the centres of, say, five wafers with it, one after the other: repeat as necessary. Be careful to let the treated wafers dry before putting them into the ciborium that is kept in an aumbry. You can then take as many wafers as you require for your round, each with a small centre spot of wine. The words used in the administration are: 'The body and blood of Christ . . .'. If communicants are few in number, perhaps it is better to use a private communion set and keep wafers and wine separate, but where numbers are large the method I have described is far easier. I used to communicate as many as forty or fifty patients before breakfast in one large hospital, using this method. Where an aumbry is used to house the reserved sacrament care must be taken to see that everything is always fresh and immaculate. The ciborium (and wine bottle if one is used) should be emptied and cleaned and refilled once a week. It is customary for a white light to be kept burning in front of the aumbry.

When private communions are held in somebody's home it is a good idea to invite relatives or possibly other church members to join in, if that is what the housebound person would like. Arrangements to be made beforehand involve providing a small table, a white cloth and perhaps a pair of candles and a small jug of water. The same arrangements are necessary if the sacrament is brought by a lay assistant straight from church.

(5) *Part-time Hospital Chaplain*

(*a*) Training

There are about 150 priests of the Church of England who

are full-time hospital chaplains and no fewer than 2,000 who hold part-time appointments. Both full-timers and part-timers are appointed by the Area Health Authority and they are legally the employers. There is an excellent publication *A Handbook on Hospital Chaplaincy* (CIO) which explains all this and much else but, curiously, makes no reference to the diocesan bishop, who would certainly expect to be consulted about part-time appointments. The part-time chaplain is usually but not invariably the parish priest. A very busy one might prefer not to take it. Whatever payment he may receive from the Area Health Authority is subtracted from his stipend augmentation grant, although some dioceses allow a scale of payment for additional responsibilities.

It is good to know that it is not now assumed that any priest can take on hospital chaplaincy duties without training. A hospital is a community of a very special kind where many professions work together and where the professionals concerned know their jobs because they have been trained to do them. Equally high standards are being demanded for chaplains. There are residential training courses arranged by the Hospital Chaplaincies Council, there are interdenominational residential training weekends, there are day or short residential courses organized by Health Regions or Areas. Incidentally neither our Church nor any other is expected to provide financial backing for these courses. The National Health Service foots the bill. These training courses are very good indeed, and every chaplain, whether full or part-time, should certainly go as opportunity offers.

(b) Terms and Conditions

Obviously it is not possible to lay down in detail what the hospital chaplain is expected to do, but guidelines are provided. He should make provision for the spiritual needs of patients and staff. He is pastor to all members of his own denomination. He should conduct services in the chapel and administer the sacrament regularly. He should visit patients and staff in the wards and in all departments and should be prepared to give special ministrations to the gravely ill or dying. He should know how to hear confessions, give the laying on of hands and anoint. He should meet all new staff members. He should co-operate with medical, nursing and administrative staff in all possible ways. He should be available to relatives of patients, especially the bereaved.

How much time ought a part-time man to devote to his hospital? Again, guidelines are provided. He is expected to put in 'sessions' of three and a half hours according to the number of patients of his denomination and the number of sessions is as follows:

Average number of patients in chaplain's denomination	Number of sessions
6–25	$\frac{1}{2}$
26–50	1
51–80	$1\frac{1}{2}$
81–120	2
121–160	$2\frac{1}{2}$
161–200	3
201–250	$3\frac{1}{2}$
251–300	4

The rule used to be that full-time chaplains could only be appointed when the average number of patients of one denomination was 750 but now the rules are more flexible. No part-time chaplain is expected to serve more than 300 patients and, where the average exceeds that, more than one part-time appointment should be made. A parish priest, before taking on part-time duty, should consider the above figures and ask himself whether he could possibly put in anything like the number of hours required. How could a busy man put in, say, fourteen hours a week unless he has a staff to assist him? In some areas, where difficulty is found in getting an incumbent or assistant curate to take on the job, a retired man is asked to do it. In many cases this works well. The retired man may well have worked for years in this capacity. He will have a wealth of experience. He may well want to put in far more than the minimum hours laid down. It should be noted that any appointment is subject to annual review after the age of seventy.

The hospital chaplain will have access as of right to much confidential information; there is now much more emphasis on this matter of confidentiality than there used to be. Apparently the fact that a person is in hospital at all is confidential! Local clergy no longer have access to admission lists. Chaplains may no longer inform a parish priest that one of his people is in hospital without that person's consent. The official argument seems to be that patients may be suffering from something that they do not want anybody to know about. After many years as a hospital chaplain I am still firmly of the opinion that many a patient wants very much to see his own parish priest, is delighted when he calls and very sad when he does not.

(c) The Duties

It is essential for the chaplain to visit every patient every week and best to have a regular day or days so that staff and patients alike know when to expect you. It is sensible to wear a name badge inscribed with your name and the words 'Hospital Chaplain', thus showing that you hold an official position. Some think a cassock should always be worn (just as a doctor always wears a white coat) in order to stress this fact. It is a good thing to begin your round with prayers in the chapel and I always did this when I had a very large hospital and there were five of us doing the visiting.

You should always call at sister's office and obtain permission to visit her ward. She (or the charge nurse) may want to tell you about particular patients and particular needs. We take care not to impose our ministrations upon those who do not want them nor do we spend too much time with those who are obviously very weak or very ill. All they may require is a quiet prayer, a laying on of hands and a blessing. You have to be perceptive to decide who wants a prayer and who would find the suggestion embarrassing. Generally (but not invariably) those who are practising Christians are grateful for a prayer. We do not have much time to stay and chat with the extroverts who are bored stiff and long to chat about everything except religion.

It is important to work closely with the staff. The consultants and doctors are busy people, but they like to get to know the chaplain. The chief nursing officer will be a friend and ally and every one I have ever known has gone out of his way to be helpful. The hospital administrator is a key figure. The medical social worker may be the most helpful ally of all. On no account should the part-time chaplain ignore the staff and think his only concern is with the patients. He should attend all social functions if possible and it is an excellent thing to have lunch with the staff in the staff canteen as frequently as possible (where incidentally you will probably get an excellent meal at a bargain price).

I always visit every patient, whereas Roman Catholic and Free Church chaplains tend to get the names of their own people and visit only them. Somehow the Anglican chaplain seems to be expected not to walk straight past any patient.

(*d*) Hospital Communions

Holy Communion is much valued by those who are regular communicants at home and some who are not. Time and again I have had people who have not received Holy Communion for years but who feel, in hospital, that this is something they want to do. Often patients who are Anglicans but who are not confirmed are given the sacrament when they tell me that when they get home they mean to be. These patients like me to get in touch with their parish priest, to pave the way for them. Any person in danger of death would certainly be given communion if this is what they wanted. I always come to an arrangement with the Free Church chaplains that their people are given communion by me when I do my weekly round and this—permitted by Canon B15A(1)—is much appreciated.

It is good to link the parish with the hospital and for years I had Mothers' Union members going around a large hospital from bed to bed collecting names. In a small hospital one keen member of the congregation did this duty and it was certainly a help. In the big hospital it seemed best to have communion at 6.45 a.m. (when all patients had been washed and the beds tidied), giving me plenty of time to end before breakfast at 7.30 a.m. In the small hospital we found 11 a.m. on Saturday mornings ideal. It is important to have the same time on the same day so that it is known you are coming.

Often mobile patients can sit around the bed of somebody who is not able to get up and sometimes sister lets staff members join in if there is not too much on. I use the card entitled The Distribution of Holy Communion from that invaluable booklet *Ministry to the Sick*. On the back of that card are forms for The Laying on of Hands and Anointing and either or both can be given after the absolution. Using the reserved sacrament, each bedside service takes only a few minutes. It is a good thing to pass on the names of Anglican communicants to their parish priests, care being taken to obtain their permission to do so.

(e) Emergency Calls

There will be emergency calls at any hour of the day or night if you make it clear to the ward sisters and night staff that you are willing to come. Ideally we ought to be sent for as are Roman Catholic priests when a faithful church member is gravely ill and death is thought to be close. When relatives of such a person are asked if they would like the chaplain to be called they very frequently answer yes.

When the Roman Catholic priest arrives he knows exactly

what to do. So should we. We are sent for to provide spiritual ministrations to both the patient and the relatives and we must therefore come with appropriate Bible readings (well-known psalms and popular hymns can be used too) and be prepared to say appropriate prayers. Both are to be found in *Ministry to the Sick*. But a word of caution is needed here. The person in danger of death may not know it. Find out from the doctor or sister about this. We must on no account terrify a patient by using commendatory prayers that suggest that death is imminent when that person has no idea his time may be very short. A lot of people do not ask a direct question because they do not want to know. There are plenty of readings and prayers suitable for such cases.

I have often been sent for to see a patient who is fully conscious but who has been told everything, including the fact that death may not be far away. There may well be relatives around the bed. I have asked to be left alone with the patient and have then asked him if he believes in God, if he accepts Jesus as Lord, if he believes in a life beyond the grave, if he has any particular worries, if there is any wrong he has committed and wants to put right. I have had many such conversations with dying people who do indeed want to get something off their chests. After this it is probably best to bring back the relatives for the readings and prayers. Sometimes you will feel it right to stay with the relatives as they keep vigil. The relatives are usually very grateful if you stay. They may be grief stricken and very frightened by what to them is something entirely new, but to you is familiar ground. By the way, my conclusion is that patients are not frightened by death. Death nearly always comes as a friend, not as an enemy. It is true however that patients, including those in no particular danger, dread the thought of pain, loss of dignity, being entirely dependent upon others and the inevitable separation that death involves. Our job is to reassure, to comfort, to encourage faith and hope. The fear is not of death but of dying. When death is near all fear seems to go—and this is not wholly due to the sedatives that are commonly given. At this time we can do far more than any doctor or nurse.

(f) Maternity Wards

If you are a part-time hospital chaplain your hospital may well contain a maternity section and if it is a large district hospital there may well be a high dependency unit attached. This will mean many emergency calls, for when a baby is very premature or when something is sufficiently wrong to require surgery it is customary for the ward sister to ask the parents if they would like the baby baptized. The answer is very frequently yes. This means calls at any time, often at night. When I had such a hospital I always went at once, saw the mother (and often the father), said a prayer with them, and then baptized the baby. The staff know just what to do about incubators and so on. There is no real problem. A shortened form of service is all that is needed (there is an excellent one in the ASB). Nursing staff should be told that they, or indeed any lay person, can baptize in an emergency and they should be shown what to do. When such baptisms occur they should always be entered into the baptism register and the parents should be told that if and when the baby recovers he should be properly received into the Church. I used to keep the register in the porter's lodge. I always informed the local incumbent after a baptism, so that he could call.

What is the point of such baptisms? Sometimes the motive is fear, sometimes desperate hope, sometimes a feeling that no ultimate salvation is possible for somebody dying unbaptized, sometimes a vague impression that a Christian funeral might be refused. I always went when sent for, not because I thought the baptism was necessary but in order to comfort the distressed parents. Time and again, before the baptism, I have spent time with them. Often they are very young and in a state of near-despair. Obviously this is no time to dispute theological niceties. The job is to comfort and sustain. Prayers in such circumstances are always warmly welcomed and the actual baptism can be regarded as doing something positive. The chaplain, in the circumstances described, may well be able to do more than anybody else to help those who feel the bottom may be dropping out of their world.

When visiting small maternity hospitals, going from bed to bed, I find a query about whether the intention is to have the baby baptized in due course makes a good beginning to what can be a useful conversation. As a matter of interest, I still find in 1984 that the great majority of mums really do want baptism for their babies. I just hope that their clergy at home will see their requests as pastoral opportunities.

(*g*) Church Services

Duties laid down include conducting services of public worship, but this is sometimes difficult (when, for instance, the chapel is well away from the wards and few patients are mobile enough to attend). Some clergy conduct services actually in the ward, with maybe a piano accompanying the hymns. These, though appreciated by some, are certainly not found at all helpful by others. They form a captive audience. There is no escape. I greatly dislike taking such services.

There are other ways. Hospitals commonly have a local radio service and the chaplain can take an interest in it and record a service every week (on any convenient day) for transmission on Sunday. Then every patient who cares to do so can turn on the head-set. It is a good thing to mention patients or staff by name, to encourage patients to choose the hymns (you can get dozens on records or tapes or record your own) and to have a discussion spot answering questions patients have actually asked.

There is another and even better way, and that is to involve the parish. You can arrange to have a British Telecom landline from church to hospital radio station and transmit your church service in full every Sunday morning. Your local manager will gladly discuss the idea. A fairly expensive installation in church is needed. You will need an amplifier and microphones at your stall, the lectern, the pulpit and the altar. You will want a telephone for direct communication with the hospital radio station and there must be a pilot loudspeaker in church to show that all is going well. The Area Health Authority must be consulted but you can expect enthusiastic approval—and maybe the League of Hospital Friends will help with the initial expenses. Naturally you make several references to the patients during the service and in the sermon you will have them very much in mind.

(h) Involving the Parish

Where the part-time chaplain is a parish priest there is one great advantage that a full-time man or a retired one does not have. He can involve the parish. The relay of the main Sunday service is one of the best ways of doing this and both members of the congregation and some patients appreciate this very much.

There are other ways. I had members of my congregation visiting the wards one afternoon a week to collect names for Holy Communion. Often a rota of lay assistants can be made, people who will come with you in the early mornings and do much to help get things ready. Members of the congregation can visit particular patients at your request, often people who receive very few visitors, even none at all. The church choir can visit the wards and sing carols at Christmas and other things at other times. The parish can arrange private hospitality schemes for relatives of those gravely ill, a good deed that can greatly help somebody. Car drivers can take out patients for an occasional drive, a service particularly appreciated where there are geriatric wards.

Nurses, particularly young student nurses, can be drawn into the life of the parish, can be welcomed in church and can count on making friendships. In the parish prayer groups patients can be prayed for by name if this is what they would like. I often had good cause to be thankful for a supportive parish when I was part-time chaplain of a very large hospital.

(6) *The Elderly and Frail*

Every parish has its elderly and frail, with their distinctive needs and problems; the number is steadily growing as people live longer. When I was a young curate their needs were given top priority at the weekly staff meeting and my rector saw to it that all the housebound were visited every week without fail, with prayers and Bible readings and regular communions.

Now the clergy are so much thinner on the ground, the elderly and frail tend to receive many less visits. But lay pastoral ministry is coming to the fore more and more, and here is one very obvious opportunity for such initiative. Every housebound old person who is a former church attender should have a member of the congregation, one or more, paying a regular weekly visit, bringing perhaps a copy of the weekly newsletter, bringing news of what is happening in the parish, making it clear that the old person is still a valued member of the church family. Regular Sunday communion can be brought by licensed administrators.

There is something else that might be considered. In some parishes tape recorders are put to good use. There may be scores of such recorders in the parish, often owned by young people, and I know of parishes where the practice is to make a recording of an actual church service and to take it around to anybody who would like to hear it. True, radio and TV provide wonderful opportunities for the housebound and frail—but many of them infinitely prefer to hear their own service from their own church.

There is something else that might be considered. In my Guildford parish we had a redundant mission church and hall. We pulled down both and built on the site a splendid block containing thirty-two single flats, four doubles, a chapel, a large lounge and a warden's flat. The scheme worked magnificently from the start. We had an avalanche of applications, mostly from locals but plenty from farther afield. We held church services in the chapel every Sunday (the chapel and hall became a splendid church on Sundays), 8 a.m. Holy Communion and 6 p.m. Evensong, and we had to make an important decision. Would we take only people who would appreciate and make use of these facilities, or ought housing need to be the main criterion? On the whole, we thought it best to give priority to those who would make use of the unique facilities we offered. After all, there were plenty of local council housing projects for the elderly without chapels or services.

The sick, the frail, the elderly and the housebound all have their special needs. Much is done to meet those needs by the welfare state but people have a right to expect the local church to be a caring community. Probably the church is judged by those outside it by the way it measures up to responsibilities of this sort.

Chapter 12

Church Buildings

(1) *Who Cares?*

'The Country Parson hath a special care of his Church, that all things there be decent and befitting his name by which it is called. Therefore, first, he takes order, that all things be in good repair; as walls plastered, windows glazed, floors paved, seats whole, firm and uniform, especially that the pulpit, and desk, and communion table and font be as they ought, for those great duties that are performed in them. Secondly that the Church be swept, kept clean, without dust or cobwebs . . .' so wrote George Herbert.

Whose responsibility is it today? If your parish has adopted the committee system for running its PCC, the church buildings committee and in particular its chairman, will take on these tasks. They should keep a vigilant eye on every church building in the parish, bringing forward proposals promptly if repairs or improvements are needed; they should keep insurance policies under regular review and ensure fire precautions are adequate; they should also make sure that everything is clean and suitable for its purpose.

The incumbent also has some responsibility, if only as the technical owner of the church. This ownership may not mean very much in legal terms but where the buildings are grubby or in poor repair, the one man who is certain to be blamed is the incumbent.

(2) *The Insurance Policies*

The new incumbent should make a point of checking the insurance policies, almost certainly issued by the Ecclesiastical Insurance Office, Beaufort House, Brunswick Road, Gloucester GL1 1JZ. They will usually send (if requested) a qualified representative to examine all the parish policies with you and your church officers and make useful suggestions to reduce risks of fire, theft and damage.

Adequate cover against the risks of fire or damage is required, with an itemized policy including the church itself, the organ, the plate and every item of furniture that is at risk. Cover against legal liability for the public and for church workers should be taken out and a special one for personal accident to voluntary workers. Every building belonging to the parish must be adequately covered. Each diocese now 'owns' the parsonage houses and will have a composite policy with the Ecclesiastical Insurance Office covering all normal risks. No further action by the PCC is necessary.

Some dioceses have gone very carefully into the question of one composite policy covering every church and every church building in the diocese. Where this can be done, the savings to the various parishes can be as high as 30 per cent; but unfortunately there are difficulties. Some parishes are hopelessly under-insured. Until they are all brought up to the required standard no diocesan composite policy is likely to be possible.

(3) *The Church Hall*

A good church hall adjoining the church is almost essential for the effective running of the parish; a hall even only a quarter of a mile away is not nearly as useful. If there is no hall adjoining the church, thought should be given to building one. Perhaps the parsonage garden or the church-yard can provide the necessary area. In several cases a most adequate church hall has been built in a closed churchyard. The legal and financial difficulties are considerable but they are not insuperable. Non-churchgoing parishioners are the most likely to object. The price of erecting a quality building is likely to be high but the money may be raised from the sale of an old hall or some other redundant church building.

Another way is to convert part of an over-large church into a hall area. Often a Victorian church seats far more people than normally attend and I have seen one aisle converted into an admirable hall area, complete with kitchen and toilet facilities. Sometimes the back of a church can be utilized in this way. In both cases planning permission will be needed—and in both cases there is likely to be vociferous opposition from non-churchgoers. It is extraordinary that such people should object to something which the incumbent and PCC feel would add to pastoral effectiveness.

(4) *Redundant Churches*

Some parish churches are no longer needed. In a large town, in these days of improved communication, it is wasteful to have to heat, light and maintain any buildings that are not really required. Sometimes people have moved away, sometimes new buildings have been erected. It often happens that a church is no longer required.

The procedure for declaring a church redundant was straightforward under the terms of the Pastoral Measure of 1968, but experience revealed that certain improvements were needed; hence the Pastoral Measure 1983 now in operation.

Every diocese now has a pastoral committee that may formulate proposals for pastoral reorganization, including declaring churches redundant. The bishop, if he agrees, forwards them to the Church Commissioners, who prepare a draft pastoral scheme that is widely publicized. Then it may be sealed by the Commissioners and confirmed by the Privy Council. If a church has been declared redundant by the scheme, it becomes the responsibility of the diocesan board of finance, and the diocesan redundant churches uses committee tries to find a suitable new use for it. It has to report to the Church Commissioners when it has found a use—or decided it cannot find one. Then the Church Commissioners redundant churches committee decides on the future of the church. There are four courses of action open to the Commissioners:

1. To appropriate the church to a suitable use.
2. If no use can be found and if the advisory board so recommend, the church may be placed in the care of the Redundant Churches Fund.
3. If neither of these courses is adopted the building can remain in the care of the diocesan board of finance.
4. If none of these courses is adopted the church has to be demolished.

The Redundant Churches Fund is financed by Church and State. In 1983 the Fund was responsible for 180 churches, and it generally acquires about twelve churches each year. The total finance likely to be available for the five years from April 1984 will be more than £6 million. There is a splendid summary of the alternative uses for redundant churches actually in operation in the Church Commissioners Annual Report 1982. They include day centre for the elderly, concert hall, art gallery and museum, county record office, village hall, diocesan treasury, craft workshop, theatre, worship by other Christian bodies and monuments.

(5) *Sharing Churches*

If there is any possibility of sharing the church building with other denominations, then this is of the greatest value. The Sharing of Church Buildings Act 1969 has removed the legal difficulties, but it is sensible to get copies of model forms of agreement and other necessary information from the Churches Main Committee, Fielden House, Little College

Street, London SW1P 3JZ. Particular attention should be paid to this possibility when the matter of church facilities for a new housing complex is under consideration.

In practical terms, it is suggested that reference should be made to *Guidelines to the Sharing of Church Buildings Act 1969*, a booklet prepared by the British Council of Churches in consultation with the Churches Main Committee. It can be obtained from the British Council of Churches, Edinburgh House, 2 Eaton Gate, London SW1W 9BL. Any serious difficulties of a financial character arising from a possible sharing agreement might be referred to the Churches Main Committee for advice.

It should be noted that the Churches which may enter into a sharing agreement include the Church of England, the Roman Catholic Church and all the principal Free Church bodies. Any two or more of such Churches may enter into a sharing agreement. Obviously the bishop, the diocesan board of finance, the pastoral committee, the incumbent and the PCC will all have their say, as well as the appropriate authorities of the other Church or Churches.

(6) *The Care of Churches*

The actual care of the parish church ought to be a major concern of any incumbent, for if he cares hardly at all then few others will show much concern. In very few cases need the incumbent be church cleaner, boilerman and grass cutter because in virtually every parish people can be found to do these necessary chores on a paid or voluntary basis. The more people who can be involved in doing jobs for the church the better.

The incumbent (or perhaps the lay rector if there is one) is the legal owner of the building and the churchwardens are responsible for the furnishings. Canon F13(1) requires that 'the churches and chapels in every parish shall be decently kept and from time to time, as occasion may require, shall be well and sufficiently repaired'. The Inspection of Churches

Measure 1955 requires every church to be inspected by an architect once in every five-year period. This architect is chosen by the PCC and approved as suitable by the diocesan advisory committee. Canon F13(4) requires that a log book shall be kept recording details of all work carried out (published by the Church Information Office). The archdeacon or rural dean is required by Canon F18 to survey each church once every three years, to see that inspections are made and repairs carried out.

There is a whole series of publications on the general subject of the Care of Churches published by the Church Information Office, all written by experts, and reference should be made to them before embarking on any of the major projects some of them deal with. Here they are:

How to Look After Your Church (An illustrated handbook containing all the essential information)

A Guide to Church Inspection and Repair (Information and advice on the quinquennial inspection of churches)

It Won't Happen to Us! (Illustrated guide to church insurance)

Lighting and Wiring of Churches (Aesthetic, practical and technical problems)

Sound Amplification in Your Church

Heating Your Church

Stonework: Maintenance and Surface Repair

Redecorating Your Church

The Churchyards Handbook (Advice on care and maintenance).

These important publications are definitive works but few PCCs will want to purchase the lot. It is better to purchase ones likely to help future projects.

I well recall that *How to Look After Your Church*, first published many years ago, contained an invaluable check-list that I trust will always reappear. Here it is:

January: Check all gutters, downpipes and gullies visually.
February: Clear concealed valleys (if any). Check inventory.
March: Re-check gutters, downpipes and gullies (with ladder and bucket of water). Make full inspection of church for Annual Parochial Church Meeting report.
April: Check bird-proofing in tower. Sweep out tower. Cut any ivy starting to grow around walls. Spray dry area to discourage weed growth.
May: Check interior for active furniture beetle, and treat. Wash windows inside and out (with soap, not detergent). Check ventilators.
June: Cut grass in churchyard. Spring-clean church.
July: Cut grass in churchyard. Cut ivy on trees.
August: Nil
September: Cut grass in churchyard. Check heating apparatus, clean flues. Inspect tower and other roofs and make sure lead-work is watertight and gutters clean.
October: Check gutters, downpipes and gullies (with ladder and bucket of water). Rod out drain runs and ensure all are clearing easily.
November: Clear the dry area and any rubbish from ventilation holes inside and out. Inspect roofs.
December: Check all gutters, downpipes and gullies visibly.
Every second year: Have lighting installation tested.
Every fifth year: Lubricate bells with special lubricant. Treat all accessible woodwork with preservatives (eaves, doors, belfry), arrange routine repainting of all external paintwork, including gutters, stay irons, tie-rod ends and iron railings. Have lightning conductor tested.

All this is of course a counsel of perfection. Who on earth would you find to do anything like all these things? I can only say that when you have a church buildings committee that includes workers as well as talkers there is no difficulty about getting quite a high proportion of the suggested jobs done.

(7) *Major Restoration Work*

Full details of all proposed major restoration work with all plans and specifications, should be sent to the diocesan advisory committee, who will advise whether a faculty or an archdeacon's certificate is required. All work except minor maintenance needs one or the other. An archdeacon's certificate will be issued only for minor repairs and redecoration; for large scale works a faculty from the chancellor of the diocese is required. For either the certificate or a faculty, the approval of the diocesan advisory committee is necessary and in both cases, under the procedure laid down in the Faculty Jurisdiction Measure 1964, parishioners must be given the opportunity to object.

When all necessary consents have been secured, tenders should be obtained from builders by the architect. It is usual to invite only builders recommended by him and accordingly it is likely that the lowest tender will be accepted. Money in the fabric fund accumulated over preceding years should be sufficient to meet the cost of the proposed work, though this is not usually the case. Money will have to be paid out as work proceeds; the architect will issue certificates from time to time stating how much is due. It is necessary to plan cash requirements in advance and to arrange an overdraft to meet the cheques while the money is being raised.

(8) *Church Heating*

Church heating has usually been installed on the cheap and putting a defective system right is often a formidable task. It is best to call in a heating engineer.

The comfort of a person in church is achieved not by adding heat but by avoiding excessive loss. In a large building thought should be given to providing at least a low level of heating throughout the heating season, so that wall surfaces never become completely chilled. Draughts are a matter for serious concern and much can be done to reduce them, such as placing fan convectors at floor level beneath the windows or hot water heaters beneath the windows or electrical tubular heaters on the window sills. The cost of the installation of a new system must be considered along with the cost of fuel and perhaps labour. A decision has to be made whether the new system should use solid fuel, liquid fuel, gaseous fuel or electricity. *Heating Your Church* (CIO) is particularly helpful. It really is an unwise economy to reduce heating costs so that only the toughest can attend services in winter.

(9) *Monumental Brasses*

If your church contains monumental brasses, you will almost certainly get many requests from people of all ages and many nationalities who want to take rubbings. Brass rubbing is a popular hobby and one can see why. The brasses themselves are often fascinating because they faithfully portray the civilian, military or ecclesiastical costume of the various periods. The actual rubbing is quite an easy process and the hobby takes an enthusiast to all kinds of beautiful buildings in pleasant parts of the country.

There are dangers in giving permission to all and sundry to take rubbings: the brass itself can suffer damage. The CIO used to publish a booklet called *Monumental Brasses and Brass Rubbing* that painted a rather alarming picture. It recommended that the incumbent and PCC should fix a fee for one rubbing for a private collection, with a greatly increased charge for further rubbings. If this is to be the parish policy, a notice should be posted stating that the brass can only be rubbed after written permission and the payment of a fee to the PCC.

Brasses should never be cleaned with metal polish. If they are dirty or corroded they should be cleaned by a weekly rub with a soft cloth soaked in paraffin. If a brass is stolen (a not unlikely eventuality) the police should at once be informed. Nowadays it is possible to have plastic copies made of all brasses and there are brass rubbing centres where many famous brasses can be rubbed without doing the surfaces any harm at all.

(10) *The Churchyard*

The church may well possess a churchyard, either closed for burials or still in use. As with churches, the incumbent is usually the owner, but this does not give him any particular rights other than the curious one of herbage. The duty of maintaining it belongs to the PCC, who must ensure that everything is kept in good order. Just as a jewel can be spoiled by a poor setting, so a fine parish church can look uncared for and unloved if the surroundings are a wilderness.

If the churchyard is old it may well be closed, no burials being permitted because it is full. A churchyard may be declared closed by an Order in Council. Under the Burial Act of 1855 maintenance can be transferred from the PCC to the local authority, although ownership remains with the incumbent. The actual procedure for doing this has been superseded by the Local Government Act 1972 (section 2150), which applies everywhere except in the City of London. Now, if a churchyard has been declared closed, the PCC may serve a written request on the local authority to take over its maintenance, and the liability for maintenance passes from the PCC to the local authority three months after it has been served. This should mean that the local authority cuts all the grass, keeps the walls and fences in a sound condition and the railings painted. Sometimes the local authority will even repair broken graves. Some local authorities take very great trouble while others are far less particular.

In some parishes the closed churchyard has been cleared of grave stones and made into a park-like area with seats. A faculty is necessary for this to be done and opportunity must be given for anybody to raise objections. Under the Pastoral Measure buildings can be erected in churchyards, provided either that there has been no burial in the proposed building site for fifty years or, if there has been, that no relative objects.

Parishioners and people dying in the parish have a right of burial where the graveyard is open. The incumbent can authorize the erection of a suitable monument but if anything about the design of the monument or the proposed wording on it worries him he can insist on a faculty being obtained. Artificial flowers should be forbidden. Whatever rules are made, undertakers and stonemasons should be made aware of them. Care should be taken to study the diocesan chancellor's regulations.

Thought might be given to providing a Garden of Remembrance in the churchyard for the interring of cremated ashes. It is certainly not Christian practice to scatter ashes, a messy and undignified business. At crematoria ashes are often scattered around rose bushes, in others they are properly interred. It is appreciated by parishioners if a Garden of Remembrance is established in the churchyard, particularly if small commemorative stones are allowed. Sometimes a Book of Remembrance is placed in a special glass-topped case in the parish church and one page turned daily. The book should contain only names and dates.

(11) *The Parsonage House*

One of the church buildings is, of course, the parsonage house and the incumbent is the owner. He is not free to make substantial alterations, fell trees and the like but he still has a duty to keep the house and garden in a good state. Incumbents who are not keen gardeners and perhaps rather short of money have a habit sometimes of just letting the garden revert to jungle; this is surely unfair to the man's successor. Under the old Dilapidations Measure the house had to be inspected and repaired every five years but all that ended in 1974. The Repair of Benefice Buildings Measure 1972 removes the responsibility from the incumbent and transfers it to the diocese. Each diocese decides how much money is needed for the upkeep of parsonage houses and how to collect it. Each parish pays an amount related to income and not to the size of the house. Thus you have an anomaly. Some incumbents and some PCCs insist on keeping the old mansion-like parsonage house and five-acre garden (with glass-houses, stables and the like) because villagers have used it all for so long and the vicar and his family have grown used to it and don't want the nuisance of moving. But this simply won't do. It is grossly unfair for such a parish to take a huge share of the available money for one house, to the detriment of all the others.

Some PCCs give generous help towards the cost of interior decoration and improvements; it is a good rule for incumbent and PCC to see that one room in the parsonage house is redecorated each year, thus saving an immense bill when a new man is appointed.

There may also be a curate's house or flat which is not subject to the Repair of Benefice Buildings Measure. PCCs would be well advised to put aside an annual sum, to arrange for a five-yearly inspection by an architect and to maintain the house in first-class order. If there is a cottage for the verger the same principle applies. So often little is done for year after year. Ultimately a huge sum of money has to be found.

Chapter 13

Ecumenism

(1) 'Our Unhappy Divisions'

The basic proposition before us when we consider ecumenism is well expressed by the Lund declaration: 'Our churches should act together in all matters except those on which deep differences of conviction compel them to act separately.' The bishops at Lambeth in 1968 endorsed this: 'whatever can be done together should be done together'. The great fact of Church life in the eighties is that this is precisely what is happening on ever widening scales. In this chapter we will look briefly at the causes of what the Prayer Book calls 'our unhappy divisions', see what has been done to mend them and look at what is permitted by law and what the various churches, including our own, now allow.

(2) *Definition of Terms*

Intercommunion Today (Report of the Archbishops' Commission on Intercommunion, Church Information Office, 1968) gives definitions that must still be considered authoritative. *Full Communion* involves mutual recognition of members and ministers, so that clergy of one Church can act in and for the other. It refers to Churches in different areas. *Organic Union* refers to churches in the same area and involves visible and corporate unity. *Unity* means communion of spirit, which is manifest in many ways, including our baptism. *Union* is defined as the relationship which results from corporate decisions between Churches. *Partial Communion* describes the various degrees of relationship which lie between the unity of Christians in Christ and the unity embodied in organic union or full communion. *Reciprocal Intercommunion* is an occasional and reciprocal sharing in the Eucharist by members of Churches which are seeking, but have not yet achieved, full communion or organic union. *Open Communion* means one particular Church welcomes all baptized communicant members of other Churches to receive communion. *Free Communion* is the practice of inviting to the Lord's Table 'all who love the Lord Jesus' whether they are baptized or not.

Concelebration refers to celebrants of the same Communion celebrating together; in episcopal Churches it requires the bishop or his representative to preside and act as chief celebrant. *Intercelebration* means parallel celebration where the ministers celebrate simultaneously but administer only to the laity of their own communion; this must happen when a Roman Catholic celebrant and his people take part.

(3) *Open Communion*

It should be widely known that the failure of the Anglican/Methodist scheme (which caused so much disappointment) and the failure of the Covenanting for Unity scheme (which caused further disappointment) did nothing to slow down the ecumenical movement. Both schemes were thrown out not because members of General Synod did not want unity but because many thought both these schemes would be divisive. During the many years of discussion relations between individual Anglican and Free Churches became close and cordial; there never has been any question of going back. There was one very valuable fruit. What previously had been the Evangelical practice of open communion became far more general.

When Professor Geoffrey Lampe moved his famous amendment to Canon B15 it was passed by a majority that surprised the more conservative. Canon B15A ('Of the Admission to Holy Communion') reads as follows:

1. There shall be admitted to the Holy Communion:

   (a) Members of the Church of England who have been confirmed in accordance with the rites of that Church or are ready and desirous to be so confirmed or who have been otherwise episcopally confirmed with unction or with the laying on of hands, except as provided by the next following Canon;

   (b) baptized persons who are communicant members of other Churches which subscribe to the doctrine of the Holy Trinity, and who are in good standing in their own Church;

   (c) any other baptized persons authorized to be admitted under regulations of the General Synod; and

   (d) any baptized person in immediate danger of death.

2. If any person by virtue of sub-paragraph (b) above regularly receives the Holy Communion over a long period which appears likely to continue indefinitely, the minister shall set before him the normal requirements of the Church of England for communicant status in that Church.

3. Where any minister is in doubt as to the application of this Canon, he shall refer the matter to the bishop of the diocese or other ordinary and follow his guidance thereon.

Any ecumenically-minded incumbent can welcome to his communion services any communicant members of other Churches. He has always been free to make his communion in any other Church (except Roman Catholic), although this was not commonly known. He can join the local Ministers' Fraternal if there is one or start one if there is not. These Fraternals usually include ministers of every denomination and in recent years Roman Catholic priests have been playing an increasingly prominent part.

(4) *Councils of Churches*

(a) Local Councils

Local Councils of Churches are very useful clearing grounds for discussion and action and some are very lively indeed. They consist of clergy and laity, and Roman Catholics often take part. If they do, it is sometimes a fact that some Pentecostal, Evangelical and Baptist churches prefer not to join in, but it is not unknown for them to change their minds when real results and growth in co-operation are seen very clearly.

The local Council should cover an identifiable geographical area which has some sense of being a community. Representatives are expected to report back to PCC's and Church Councils, who can themselves suggest ideas to the local Council. The clergy simply must join. It does not do to leave it all to the laity, because it gives the impression that the clergy regard it as unimportant if they are not seen there.

What sort of things can a Council do? Suggestions from the British Council include the following:

Arrange joint youth weekends.

Plan courses of study (possibly in house groups).

Do Christian Aid Week collecting.

Develop drop-in centres for the unemployed, lunch clubs for the elderly, coffee bars for young people.

Explore the possibilities of local radio and phone-in programmes.

Work out imaginative schemes for the better observance of the Week of Prayer for Christian Unity.

Consider possible co-operation with the local authority or with voluntary bodies.

Stage a Good Friday Pageant in the local shopping centre.

Look at the possibilities of using video, for education perhaps, or for use with the housebound.

Councils of Churches everywhere support the Week of Prayer for Christian Unity and Christian Aid Week.

(*b*) The British Council of Churches

Every Council of Churches is affiliated to or associated with the British Council of Churches and so obtains a broader view of the whole unity movement. The British Council of Churches, inaugurated in 1942, is a fellowship of Churches in the British Isles which 'confess the Lord Jesus Christ as God and Saviour according to the Scriptures and therefore seek to fulfil together their common calling to the glory of the one God, Father, Son and Holy Spirit'. There are twenty-seven member Churches, of which sixteen have their headquarters in England, five in Scotland, three in Ireland, and three in Wales. Associate members include the Society of Friends and the Unitarians. The Roman Catholic Church and the Seventh-Day Adventists have consultant/observer status.

The programme of the British Council is carried out mainly through five divisions, which are:

1. Christian Aid (Income in 1982, c.£8m. of which 87 per cent was spent on work overseas, 7 per cent on education and community relations projects and 4 per cent on overseas students. Very little was spent on administration.)
2. Conference for World Mission. (A forum for consultation and joint action by thirty-seven member missionary societies and boards. It is also concerned with relations with people of other faiths.)
3. Division of Community Affairs. (Currently concerned with poverty, information technology, nationality legislation and opportunities for voluntary social work.)
4. Division of Ecumenical Affairs. (This helps member Churches to work, think and pray together in the interlocking areas of unity, renewal and mission.)
5. Division of International Affairs. (It identifies and examines world issues.)

(*c*) The World Council of Churches

The British Council of Churches is an Associated National Council of the World Council of Churches. The World

Council of Churches was brought into being in 1948. In an amended constitution, accepted by the Nairobi Assembly in 1975, the functions of the Council are as follows:

1. To call the Churches to the goal of visible unity in one faith and in one eucharistic fellowship expressed in worship and in common life in Christ, and to advance towards that unity in order that the world may believe.
2. To facilitate the common witness of the Churches in each place and in all places.
3. To support the Churches in their world-wide missionary and evangelistic task.
4. To express the common concern of the Churches in the service of human need, the breaking down of barriers between people, and the promotion of one human family in justice and peace.
5. To foster the renewal of the Churches in unity, worship, mission and service.
6. To establish and maintain relations with national councils and regional conferences of Churches, world confessional bodies and other ecumenical organizations.
7. To carry on the work of the world movements for Faith and Order and Life and Work and of the International Missionary Council and the World Council of Christian Education.

All this sounds (and undoubtedly is) most valuable and important and worthy of support. But it is fair to say that the World Council of Churches does not commend itself very widely to the Church of England as a whole, especially to those of right-wing political views. The 1983 World Congress at Vancouver failed to censure the Soviet Union for its invasion of Afghanistan (in response to earnest pleas from the Russian Orthodox bishops who were present) but strongly condemned the USA and Great Britain and other 'have' nations for gross selfishness and of course came down like a ton of bricks upon South Africa. The World Council is obviously Third World orientated and it is difficult to see

how it can be any other. Left-wing clergy and laity may
strongly support it but others reserve the right to disapprove
of, e.g., grants to so-called freedom fighters.

(5) *Local Ecumenical Projects*

This term replaces what used to be called Areas of
Ecumenical Experiment. Local ecumenical projects are one
of the most important recent developments in our Church
life. There were, in 1983, about 300 of them and the number is
growing. How does a local ecumenical project start? The
members of at least two Christian congregations decide to
work closely together. They do so because they are
convinced that this will help the Church to serve the local
area better. It does not involve starting a new denomination.
Each denomination must give its approval and there must be
a Sponsoring Body, i.e. a group appointed by the denominations to keep an eye on things and give advice and support.
Member churches keep their own ministers but see more of
other ministers. Members will probably keep their own
familiar services but have some new ones too. Existing
buildings will probably be kept but some may be put to
better use and some may be closed.

  For those who want more information, there is now a
Consultative Committee for Local Ecumenical Projects in
England, known as CCLEPE. There is a leaflet called *What
is CCLEPE?* and another called *What is a Sponsoring Body?*
and a third called *What is a Local Ecumenical Project?* All
these can be obtained from the British Council of Churches, 2
Eaton Gate, London SW1 9BL. Obviously many local
ecumenical projects will involve shared churches. This
subject had better have a section all to itself.

(6) *Sharing Churches*

All necessary details of the Sharing of Church Buildings Act
1969 will be found in *A Handbook for Churchwardens and*

Parochial Church Councillors (Mowbray, 1983). Sharing may be of two sorts; the buildings may remain the property of one denomination, or they may be jointly owned. In each case, there must be trustees and an agreement about finances. The Act insists that no new denomination arises from the sharing, so the participants must have their own distinctive services. In many cases, however, there is a good deal of coming together by the sharing church members. The only surprise to some of us is that in some areas the Churches insist on going it alone. The mounting costs for repairs and upkeep and heating surely indicate that sharing is something to be explored. Of course there are legal and practical difficulties but these can usually be overcome. Much welcome guidance will be found in *Guidelines to the Sharing of Church Buildings Act 1969* (British Council of Churches). In 1983 the Church of England and the Methodist Church were involved in more than 200 shared buildings, the United Reformed Church in over 150, the Baptists in around fifty and the Roman Catholic Church in just under fifty. Those who want more detailed information can obtain it from the Ecumenical Officer for England, British Council of Churches, 2 Eaton Gate, London SW1W 9BL. There are further broadsheets issued from time to time. *The Bristol Handbook for Local Ecumenical Projects* is valuable. There is also *TAP*, a bulletin of news for teams and projects, and occasional papers called *Tap Roots*.

(7) *The Roman Catholic Church*

No scheme for unity that leaves out the Roman Catholic Church is likely to be acceptable to a great many Anglicans. There is plenty to encourage in recent years. The *ARCIC Agreed Statement on the Eucharist*, containing the results of intense discussion that took place at Windsor as long ago as 1971 (it was published by SPCK), revealed a very substantial measure of doctrinal agreement and hopes were high that at last there might be a break-through in the matter of unity.

But the *ARCIC* statement was never accepted officially by anybody. We ought not to be in any kind of doubt. The official Roman Catholic view is still that our orders are not valid and our sacraments not genuine. An official statement by the Catholic Bishops of England and Wales, called *The Easter People* and published in 1980, affirms existing disapproval of intercommunion, adding the ominous words: 'We are unable to compromise these principles'.

Rome regards intercommunion as a fruit of unity achieved and not as a means to that end. But it ought not to be supposed that barriers are still as formidable as they used to be. There now exists ecumenical co-operation that only a few years ago would have seemed impossible. Roman Catholic priests invite their Anglican counterparts to take part in mixed marriage ceremonies and are willing to share in an Anglican service in an Anglican church. Joint study groups and joint activities abound. The official view that our orders are invalid is clearly not shared by many a Roman Catholic priest, whatever the hierarchy may say.

The present position is roughly as follows. The admission of non-Catholics to communion is permitted for people 'in danger of death or in urgent need'. Christians in 'grave spiritual necessity' and particularly non-Catholics scattered in Catholic regions with no priest of their own may also qualify, though not yet in England. Mixed marriages are not forbidden but are certainly not encouraged. The Catholic party incurs an obligation to safeguard his own faith and also, as far as possible, to have children of the marriage brought up as Catholics (although no formal promise is required). There is evidence that in mixed marriages individual Roman Catholic priests admit the non-Catholic partner to communion but one imagines this is done without reference to the bishop for guidance. Every bishop can only say no. There is an interesting book on the whole subject of mixed marriages in this country called *Sharing Communion* (edited by Ruth Reardon and Melanie Funch, Collins, 1983) that contains full documentation and reflects the grief, bewilderment and positive anger voiced by some Anglicans who refuse to change Churches.

Some Catholics can and do co-operate with us, attend Council of Churches meetings, share church buildings and no longer appear to be intent on making converts. It is surely reasonable to suppose that before very long Anglican orders will be recognized as valid.

A very significant paper called *Local Churches in Covenant* was published in 1983 after approval by the Roman Catholic Bishops of England and Wales and outlines possible approaches to local unity. Covenanting for unity is warmly welcomed, provided the sharing of communion is left out. The paper can be obtained from Catholic Information Services, 74 Gallows Hill Lane, Abbots Langley, Herts WD5 0BZ.

Chapter 14

Outside the Parish

(1) *The Deanery*

Every parish is in a deanery and the rural dean will generally hold a chapter meeting of all the clergy monthly. The rural dean is sometimes chosen by the clergy by election (as in the Truro diocese) but more often he is appointed by the bishop, who usually invites the clergy to suggest a name before he makes the final choice. The rural dean should know all the clergy in his deanery and keep the bishop informed about anything he ought to know. He will attend regular rural deans' meetings convened by the bishop and at the chapter meetings he can pass on the bishop's requests and instructions. A good rural dean will see to it that clergy wives also meet regularly.

(2) *The Deanery Synod*

The clergy meet with the laity in the deanery synod. Under the Synodical Government Measure the objects of a deanery synod are:

(a) to consider matters concerning the Church of England and to make provision for such matters in relation to their deanery, and to consider and express their opinion on any other matters of religious or public interest;
(b) to bring together the views of the parishes of the deanery

on common problems, to discuss and formulate common policies on those problems, to foster a sense of community and interdependence among those parishes and generally to promote in the deanery the whole mission of the church, pastoral, evangelistic, social and ecumenical;

(c) to make known and as far as appropriate put into effect any provision made by the diocesan synod;

(d) to consider the business of the diocesan synod and particularly any matters referred to that synod by the General Synod, and to sound parochial opinion whenever they are required or consider it appropriate to do so;

(e) to raise such matters as the deanery synod consider appropriate with the diocesan synod.

The deanery synod is elected every three years at the annual church meetings, has between 50 and 150 members and consists of a house of clergy and a house of laity. Deanery synods also act as an electorate for the General and diocesan synods (but proctors are elected by the clergy beneficed and licensed in the diocese).

(3) *The Diocesan Synod*

The diocesan synod is composed of three houses, i.e. a house of bishops (the diocesan, who is *exofficio* president of the synod, every suffragan and any other bishops in the diocese nominated by the diocesan), a house of clergy and a house of laity. The Measure lists the objects of diocesan synods as:

(a) to consider matters concerning the Church of England and to make provision for such matters in relation to their diocese, and to consider and express their opinion on any other matters of religious or public interest;

(b) to advise the bishop on any matters on which he may consult the synod;

(c) to consider and express their opinion on any matters referred to them by the General Synod, and in particular to approve or disapprove provisions referred to them by the General Synod under Article 8 of the Constitution.

Membership should be between 150 and 270 and membership of the houses of clergy and laity should be roughly equal. The bishop has a duty to consult with the diocesan synod on matters of general concern to the diocese. Every diocese must elect a body known as 'the bishop's council and standing committee', a very important body in every diocese, for it originates the business of the synod and obviously has great influence on diocesan policy.

(4) *The General Synod*

The objects of the General Synod are laid down in schedule 2 paragraph 6 of the Measure but the wording is legalistic jargon and needs to be improved. My friend Mr Oswald Clark, chairman of the House of Laity of the General Synod, drew up a far better list some years ago and I have his permission to quote it. He claims that the varied functions of the Synod include those of:

(a) a legislative assembly, preparing measures, canons and regulations of statutory force;
(b) a liturgical body, approving forms of service, ceremonies and versions of Scripture and dealing with matters of doctrine;
(c) a financial authority, authorizing money resolutions, approving a budget and making apportionments;
(d) an administrative organ, regulating powers and composition of 'a hierarchy' of subordinate bodies and the appointment of certain of their staffs, as well as its own;
(e) a deliberative forum, constitutionally empowered to express an opinion on any 'matters of religious or public interest'.

The General Synod consists of three houses—the house of bishops (all diocesans and the elected suffragans of both provinces), the house of clergy (all clergy elected to serve as Proctors in Convocation plus at least one archdeacon from each diocese and a number of deans elected by themselves, maximum 268 members) and the house of laity (not more than 263 members, including 250 elected by the dioceses).

The old Convocations of York and Canterbury continue to exist and indeed occasionally meet, but their powers are much curtailed. The General Synod must meet at least twice a year. The CIO publishes a very useful *Synod Report* after each session. Very full accounts will also be found in the *Church Times* and the *Church of England Newspaper*, with informed comment. The proctors and the lay representatives are often invited to address chapter meetings, deanery synods and PCC meetings.

The incumbent should concern himself with synodical government at every level, to find out what is going on and to see that his parish plays a full part. It may well be that he will feel it right to offer himself for election to the diocesan synod or to the General Synod. Membership of the General Synod is time consuming (there is an immense amount of reading required before each session) but very worthwhile. Details for standing as a candidate can always be obtained from the diocesan secretary.

(5) *The Bishop and his Officers*

The incumbent should refer all really serious problems to his diocesan bishop but he may be held back by the reflection that bishops are grossly overworked. The bishop will send out regulations from time to time and these should be carefully filed and scrupulously obeyed. The bishop will also expect to be consulted if and when the incumbent wants to move or if he faces a crisis in family or parish. If he does not feel his problem is one that only his diocesan can handle, the incumbent will probably get in touch with the suffragan bishop. Most dioceses have one or more; their chief duty is to ease the burden of work from the shoulders of the diocesan. The archdeacon may also help and advise, as he is the authority on legal procedures, on the care of buildings and parsonage matters. Archdeacons have usually had extensive parish experience, so clergy who feel discouraged and depressed often find that the archdeacon is approachable and helpful. Questions, problems, and queries of a minor nature should be referred to the rural dean. Queries about marriage licences can be dealt with by the nearest surrogate, an incumbent specially appointed by the bishop for this purpose.

(6) *Diocesan Support Facilities*

(a) The Diocesan Secretary

Nearly every diocese has a well-staffed diocesan Church House where you will find well-qualified people ready to help and advise. Chief of these is the diocesan secretary, who is likely to be secretary of the board of finance. He would probably like every new incumbent to call at Church House during his first month in the parish, so that he can be introduced to staff members and be told what they do. He will be able to answer questions about pay scales both for incumbents and assistant curates; clergy should not be embarrassed or hesitant to ask him about money matters. He is also the person to consult about housing matters, parish boundaries, or any properties held in the parish: (the deeds of all such properties will probably be in Church House). He can be consulted about quota assessments. He will also advise about the possibility of obtaining grants or loans from diocesan sources when major repairs or building works are contemplated, but he cannot help with parish records or registers since these are never in his custody.

(*b*) The Director of Education

There will probably be an education department, with a director and a Sunday school adviser. The new incumbent can look to the diocesan education department for financial, legal and practical advice if he has a church school, for help on teaching methods for his teachers and for help when dealing with his local education authority. Advice will be given on courses to use with people of all ages in voluntary groups and training courses for leaders will be arranged from time to time. Members of the education team (if there is one) will address PCCs, if invited, explaining what is being tried and used in other parishes.

(*c*) The Youth Officer

There may be a diocesan council for youth, with perhaps a youth officer or a youth chaplain; if so, it will have close links with the diocesan education department. A youth officer will be concerned with young people at home, at school, at work, in their leisure and in their personal relationships; he will visit the incumbent to consult with him, his staff or any parish organization; he will also talk to the PCC. The incumbent will receive from him notices about training schemes, leadership courses and holiday plans. He will know in what ways the local authority can help with grants and he will be well qualified to advise you if you want to set up an open or closed youth club. He will be in touch with organizations that sponsor overseas service, youth exchange visits and international conferences.

(*d*) The Director of Social Responsibility

Some dioceses have a council for social work. This used to be concerned largely with moral welfare, running mother and baby homes. This work was handed over to the local authorities many years ago. Councils for social work now maintain a close liaison with these local authorities at all levels, so that they can best serve the church and the community. They encourage clergy to involve themselves in voluntary organizations such as mental health associations, marriage guidance councils, associations for handicapped people, old people's welfare committees and so on. Clergy who feel that the Church ought to be far more concerned with people in need would do well to consult this useful council.

(e) The Canon Missioner

There may also be a canon missioner, although titles vary for this important officer. His role is to conduct parochial evangelistic missions and to minister to the clergy by spiritual direction and hearing confessions. The pattern seems to be changing: retreats and teaching conferences seem to have replaced evangelistic missions; pastoral counselling has taken the place of the confessional. The canon missioner also handles difficult pastoral cases passed on by the parochial clergy and advises them on just about everything from exorcism to deep moral problems. Parish priests are often glad to have somebody outside the parish to whom they can turn in this sort of way.

I am aware that I have listed only some of the diocesan officers. There are other very important ones such as the diocesan register, the stewardship adviser, the chairman of the council for mission and unity and the chairman of the pastoral training advisory council. There may well be others. The great thing is to get to know them and not to hesitate to refer any matters to them where you think they may be able to help.

(7) *The Local Authorities*

Every new incumbent should try to get to know the chief officers of the local authorities in whose area his parish falls.

The first one to approach is the chief executive, the general manager of the authority. It is possible that he will introduce you to his principal officers: the chief housing officer, the chief planning officer, the chief environmental health officer, the chief technical officer, the treasurer and the secretary. Anybody who wants to know in great detail the precise functions of each will find full information in *The Bains Report* (HM Stationery Office), but the titles may vary in different authorities.

(8) *Local Welfare Services*

The clergy used to be welfare specialists; anybody in any kind of trouble came first to his parish priest to see what could be done. Now the parish priest is often the last to hear about the trouble because he is judged least able to help. The clergy should get to know the staff and facilities available from the welfare departments. We are concerned with people and so are they. We may well become involved with the police, the probation service, the department of health and social security, the citizens' advice bureau and the marriage guidance council. In every case it is sensible to find out the name of the principal officer and to make an appointment to see him. The idea is to find out what sort of co-operation is likely to be useful.

It may well be that the manager of the department of health and social security will be the most valuable and most used contact of all. These officers are not remote bureaucrats; they are concerned with people in need and they are particularly concerned about the vast number of people in every area who are entitled to benefit but who do not know it; they regard the clergy as partners in the same enterprise and are almost invariably most willing to co-operate.

If you have a lot of cases of genuine need you will find in the office of the department of health and social security a wide selection of free leaflets explaining complex matters in simple language. Many of them can be obtained from any post office. We ought to know what help is available and be able to advise parishioners who are in severe straits and have no knowledge of what help is available. A booklet called *Which Benefit?* lists just about all the benefits and leaflets. It can be obtained from any local social security office or by post from DHSS Leaflets, Government Buildings, PO Box 21, Honeypot Lane, Stanmore, Middlesex HA7 1AY.

(9) *The Marriage Guidance Council*

The marriage guidance council is likely to be another very valuable ally. This excellent voluntary organization specializes in remedial work in cases of marriage difficulty but is also very willing to arrange discussion groups for engaged couples. The difficulty is getting the engaged couples to attend and it is here that the Churches can help. The council will provide lectures if numbers justify it; if not, they will almost certainly welcome young couples to courses they have themselves arranged. These will probably include such topics as money, children, family relationships, housing, sex, contraception and leisure.

(10) *Working Lunch*

In some areas all those working in the welfare field meet together for a working lunch once a week or so; clergy and social workers find this most rewarding. This arrangement seems most general in new housing areas but wherever it can be arranged, clergy should obviously take part. We can do much to smooth the path for the welfare worker though the relationship is not always easy.

(11) *The Spiritual Dimension*

The parish priest must on no account try to act alone. There was a time when he saw himself as the leader, running his own parish, making all the decisions himself. Now the synodical spirit is abroad: clergy and laity consult together about everything important. We live in ecumenical days: everything should be done with members of other Churches except where this is absolutely impossible. We live in a welfare state: parish priests are no longer the only people concerned with human problems. There are vast numbers of highly trained professionals coping with practically every known problem. We know that we can work with them.

All parish work has to be done in the name of God, to his greater glory and for the extension of his kingdom. We are entrusted with a great office. We cannot do it without the strength and wisdom that God supplies.

Bibliography

The Church of England Year Book (Church Information Office, 1984)

A Handbook For Churchwardens and Parochial Church Councillors, MacMorran, Elphinstone & E. Garth Moore (Mowbray, 1983)

A Handbook of Church Property, K. J. T. Elphinstone (Mowbray, 1973)

The Parish Comes Alive, Ernest Southcott (Mowbray, 1956)

The Parish Seeks the Way, Michael Hocking (Mowbray, 1962)

The Office and Work of a Priest, R. Martineau (Mowbray, 1980)

The Christian Priest Today, Michael Ramsey, former Archbishop of Canterbury (SPCK, 1972)

Ecclesiastical Law (Halsbury's Laws of England) (Butterworth, 1957)

Archbishops' Commissions:

Church and State (Chadwick Report) (CIO, 1970)

Marriage, Divorce and the Church (Root Report) (SPCK, 1971)

Partners in Ministry (Morley Report) (CIO, 1967)

Intercommunion Today (Tomkins Report) (CIO, 1968)

Government by Synod (Hodson Report) (CIO, 1966)

The Fourth R (Durham Report) (SPCK, 1971)

Christian Initiation (Roberts Report) (CIO, 1971)

Baptism, Thanksgiving and Blessing (Ramsey Report) (CIO, 1971)

The Bains Report (Stationery Office, 1972)

Primer for Teams, Peter Croft (ONE Publications, 1979)

TAP Handbook for Teams and Groups, John Hammersley (British Council of Churches, 1981)

Church Commissioners Report and Accounts (annual)

The Parochial Expenses of the Clergy (Central Stipends Authority, 1982)

A Theology of Generosity, W. W. Badger Berrie (Mowbray, 1981)

Tithing, R. T. Kendall (Hodder & Stoughton, 1982)

Fund Raising A to Z, Alan Robinson (Kirkfield Publications, 1982)

The Alternative Service Book 1980—a Commentary by the Liturgical Commission (CIO)

Introductions to the ASB Readings, William Collins (Mowbray, 1982)

Reflections on the Readings for Holy Communion in the ASB 1980, Dennis Page (Mowbray, 1983)

The Ministry of the Word, D. W. Cleverley Ford (Hodder & Stoughton, 1979)

I Believe in Preaching, John Stott (Hodder & Stoughton, 1982)

Guide to Magazine Production for Churches, Alan Robinson (Kirkfield Publications)

Managing the Church Bookstall (Hodder & Stoughton)

Open the Doors, Edward Patey (Mowbray, 1979)

Grow through Groups, Eddie Gibbs (Grove Books)

Family Services, Kenneth Stevenson (Alcuin Club/SPCK, 1981)

Towards Confirmation, John Eddison (Marshall, Morgan & Scott, 1982)

Confirmation Cook Book, David Manship (Mowbray, 1980)

A Pocket Guide to the Anglican Church, R. H. Lloyd (Mowbray, 1984)

Communicant's Manual, William Purcell (Mowbray, 1981, 1984)

In his Presence, Denis E. Taylor (Religious Education Press, 1982)

Children of Promise, Geoffrey Bromley (T. & T. Clark, 1979)

Christian Baptism, Philip Crowe (Mowbray, 1980)

Nuptial Blessing, Kenneth Stevenson (Alcuin Club/SPCK, 1982)

To Have and to Hold, David Atkinson (Collins, 1979)

A Handbook on Hospital Chaplaincy (CIO)

Guidelines to the Sharing of Church Building 1969 (British Council of
Churches)

Sharing Communion, ed. Ruth Reardon and Melanie Funch (Collins, 1983)

Open the Book, Edward Patey (Mowbray, 1981)

The Pastoral Nature of the Ministry, Frank Wright (SCM, 1980)

Pastoral Care for Lay People, Frank Wright (SCM, 1982)

Learning to Care, Michael H. Taylor (SPCK, 1983)

The Christian Healing Ministry, Morris Maddocks (SPCK, 1981)

Nuptial Blessing, Kenneth Stevenson (Alcuin Club/SPCK, 1982)

To Have and to Hold, David Atkinson (Collins, 1979)

I give you this ring, Edward Patey (Mowbray, 1982)

Dilemmas of Dying, Ian Thompson (Edinburgh University Press, 1979)

Troubled Water, Neil Dixon (Epworth, 1979)

All Change, Michael Saward (Hodder and Stoughton, 1983)

The Church in the Market Place, George Carey (Kingsway Publications,
1984)

Exploring Worship, Colin Hodgetts (Mowbray, 1980)

Tend my Sheep, H. Tayor (SPCK, 1983)

Liturgy Pastoral and Parochial, Michael Perham (SPCK, 1984)

Training for Diversity in Ministry (University of Nottingham, 1983)

Explorations into Parish Ministry, John Mills and John Nelson (Liverpool
Diocese, 1983)

A Strategy for the Church's Ministry, John Tiller (CIO, 1983)

Towards Confirmation, John Eddison (Marshall, Morgan and Scott, 1982)

After Confirmation, R. H. Lloyd (Mowbray, 1980)

Footholds in the Faith, Peter Moore (Mowbray, 1980)

Draw Near with Faith, Geoffrey Shilvock (Mowbray, 1984)

A Handbook of Parish Youth Work, Clive Andrews (Mowbray, 1984)

A Handbook of Sick Visiting, Norman Autton (Mowbray, 1981)

The Ministry of the World, Geoffrey Cuming (Oxford University Press,
1979)

The Recovery of Preaching, Henry H. Mitchell (Hodder & Stoughton, 1979)

The Whole Family of God, John Austin Baker (Mowbray, 1981)

Preaching at the Parish Communion ASB Gospels—Sundays: Year 1, Dennis B. Runcorn (Mowbray, 1982)

Preaching at the Parish Communion ASB Gospels—Sundays: Year 2, Raymond Wilkinson (Mowbray,1983)

Preaching at the Parish Communion ASB Epistles—Sundays: Year 1, R. O. Osborne (Mowbray, 1984)

Preaching on Special Occasions Volume 2, D. W. Cleverley Ford (Mowbray, 1982)

Preaching Through the Acts of the Apostles, D. W. Cleverley Ford (Mowbray, 1980)

Preaching Through St Paul, Derrick Greeves (Mowbray, 1980)

Preaching Through the Prophets, John B. Taylor (Mowbray, 1983)

Preaching Through the Psalms, D. W. Cleverley Ford (Mowbray, 1984)

More Preaching from the New Testament, D. W. Cleverley Ford (Mowbray, 1982)

More Preaching from the Old Testament, D. W. Cleverley Ford (Mowbray, 1983)

Preaching Through the Christian Year, Vol. 7, Alan Dunstan (Mowbray, 1980)

Preaching Through the Christian Year, Vol. 8, Frank Colquhoun (Mowbray, 1981)

Preaching Through the Christian Year, Vol. 9, Robert Martineau (Mowbray, 1983)

Useful Addresses

Additional Curates Society: St Mark's Church House, 264A Washwood
    Heath Road, Birmingham B8 2XS
Anglican Young People's Association: Chi Rho House, All Saints Vicarage,
    Compton Leek ST13 5PT
Bible Reading:
  Bible Reading Fellowship, St Michael's House, 2 Elizabeth St, London
    SW1W 9RQ
  Scripture Union, 130 City Road EC1V 2NJ
British Council of Churches: 2 Eaton Gate, Sloane Sq. London SW1W 9BL
Catholic Information Services: 74 Gallows Hill Lane, Abbots Langley,
    Herts WD5 0BZ
Central Board of Finance: Church House, Dean's Yard, London SW1P
    3NZ
Church Army Housing Association: Welford House, 112a Shirland Road,
London W9 2EL
Church Commissioners: 1 Millbank, London SW1P 3JZ
Church House Bookshop, Great Smith St, London SW1P 3BN
Church Information Office: Church House, Dean's Yard, London SW1P
    3NZ
Church Newspapers:
  Church Times, 7 Portugal St, Kingsway, London WC2A 2HP
  Church of England Newspaper, 146 Queen Victoria St EC4V 4EH
  Church News Service, 37B New Cavendish St, London W1M 8JR
Church of England Children's Society: Old Town Hall, Kennington,
    London SE11 4QD
Church of England Men's Society: 18 Hertford St, Coventry CV1 1LF
Churches Main Committee: Fielden House, Little College St, London
    SW1P 3JZ
Church Pastoral Aid Society: Falcon Court, 32 Fleet St, London EC4Y
    1DB
Church of England Pensions Board: 53 Tufton St, London SW1P 3QP
Clergy Appointments Adviser: Fielden House, Little College St, London
    SW1P 3SH
College of Preachers: St Margaret Pattens Church, Eastcheap, London
    EC3M 1HS
Ecclesiastical Insurance Office: Beaufort House, Brunswick Road,
    Gloucester GL1 1JZ
General Synod (Boards, Advisory Committees and Permanent
    Commissions):

Council for the Deaf: Church House, Dean's Yard, London SW1P 3NZ

Council for the Care of Churches: 83 London Wall, London EC2M 5NA

Doctrine Commission: c/o Church House, Dean's Yard, London SW1P 3NZ

Hospital Chaplaincies Council: Church House, Dean's Yard, London SW1P 3NZ

Legal Advisory Commission: Church House, Dean's Yard, London SW1P 3NZ

Board for Mission and Unity: Church House, Dean's Yard, London SW1P 3NZ

Board for Social Responsibility: Church House, Dean's Yard, London SW1P 3NZ

Advisory Council for the Church's Ministry: Church House, Dean's Yard, London SW1P 3NZ

Board of Education: Church House, Dean's Yard, London SW1P 3NZ

Guild of St Raphael: St Marylebone Church, Marylebone Road, London NW1 5LT

Guild of the Servants of the Sanctuary: 8 Dalefields Road, Roebuck Lane, Buckhurst Hill, Essex

Missionary Societies:

Bible Churchmen's Missionary Society, 251 Lewisham Way SE4 1XF

British and Foreign Bible Society, Bible House, 146 Queen Victoria St, London EC4V 4BX

Church Army, Independents Road, Blackheath, London SE3 9LG

Church Missionary Society, 157 Waterloo Rd, London SE1L 8UU

Missions to Seamen, St Michael Paternoster Royal, College Hill, London EC4R 2RL

Society for Promoting Christian Knowledge, Holy Trinity Church, Marylebone Rd, London NW1 4DU

South American Missionary Society, Allen Gardiner House, Pembury Road, Tunbridge Wells, Kent TN2 3QU

United Society for the Propagation of the Gospel, 15 Tufton St, London SW1P 3QQ

Mothers' Union: Mary Sumner House, 24 Tufton St, London SW1P 3RB

National Federation of Housing Associations: 30 Southampton St, London WC2

National Society for Promoting Religious Education: Church Dean's Yard, Westminster SW1P 3NZ

Insets for Parish Magazines:

The Sign, A. R. Mowbray and Co. Ltd, Oxford

Home Words and *Church News*, Home Words Printing and Publishing Co.

Compass, Compass Newspapers, 319 Gazette Building, Corporation St, Birmingham 4

Parochial Clergy Association: Rectory, Burbage, Hinckley, Leics L10 2AW

Prison Service Chaplaincy: Home Office Prison Department, Portland House, Stag Place, London, SW1E 5BX

Redundant Churches Committee: 1 Millbank, London SW1P 3JZ

Religious Broadcasting (BBC): Broadcasting House, London W1A 1AA

Religious Broadcasting (IBA): 70 Brompton Rd, London SW3

Retired Clergy Association, London Diocesan House, 30 Causton Street, London SW1P 4AU

Roman Catholic Ecumenical Commission: 42 Francis Street, London SW1P 1 QR

Royal School of Church Music: Addington Palace, Croydon CR9 5AD

Society of Genealogists: 37 Harrington Gardens, London SW7 4JX

Statistical Unit of the Board of Finance: Church House, Dean's Yard, London SW1 3NZ

Young Men's Christian Association: 640 Forest Road, London E17 EDZ

Youth Organizations:

Boys' Brigade, Brigade House, Parsons Green, London SW6 4TH

Church Lads' Brigade, Claude Hardy House, 15 Etchingham Park Rd, Finchley, London N3 3DU

Girls' Friendly Society, Townsend House, 126 Queen's Gate, London SW7 5LQ

Guides' Association, 17/19 Buckingham Palace Rd, London SW1W 0PT

Scout Association, Baden Powell House, Queen's Gate, London SW7 5JS

Index